INFORMED DIALOGUE

Using Research to
Shape Education Policy
Around the World

Fernando Reimers and Noel McGinn

Westport, Connecticut
London

Library of Congress Cataloging-in-Publication Data

Reimers, Fernando.
   Informed dialogue : using research to shape education policy
around the world / Fernando Reimers and Noel McGinn.
       p.   cm.
   Includes bibliographical references and index.
   ISBN 0–275–95442–0 (alk. paper). — ISBN 0–275–95443–9 (pbk. :
alk. paper)
   1. Education and state. 2. Education—Research. 3. Education and
state—Case studies. 4. Education—Research—Case studies.
I. McGinn, Noel F., 1934–   . II. Title.
LC71.R45 1997
379'.07'2—dc21   96–50323

British Library Cataloguing in Publication Data is available.

Library of Congress Catalog Card Number: 96–50323
ISBN: 0–275–95442–0
     0–275–95443–9 (pbk.)

First published in 1997

Praeger Publishers, 88 Post Road West, Westport, CT 06881
An imprint of Greenwood Publishing Group, Inc.

Printed in the United States of America

To Mary Lou McGinn
and Eleonora Villegas-Reimers,
Who have taught us much
about the power of dialogue

Contents

Acknowledgments

This book is the result of our reflections about our own practice as education researchers advising governments around the world. Numerous colleagues and friends have stimulated these reflections. The direct and indirect influences in our thinking about how research can best inform policy dialogue are too many to mention here, and there is no doubt that some influences have passed unperceived by us. We beg forgiveness of those colleagues we should have mentioned but have unintentionally overlooked. We have listed here colleagues and associates of recent years, during which time our understanding of the ideas expressed in this book came into focus.

We owe our biggest debt to all the colleagues and associates of the Basic Research and Implementation in Developing Education Systems (BRIDGES) project. This project, funded by the United States Agency for International Development (USAID), sponsored research activities to improve education around the world. Some of these are the core of the experience upon which the reflections contained in this book are based. We appreciate the support and collegiality of our colleagues in USAID during those years, particularly Frank Method, Jim Hoxeng, Gary Theisen, and Richard Pelczar. In the USAID field offices, we were privileged to know the late Frank Fairchild, Nadine Dutcher, and our friends, Henry Reynolds and Cynthia Rohl, who shared our interest in the practical consequences of research and in finding ways to improve the policy relevance of research and analysis. Our government counterparts and the many collaborators in the countries where we worked were also sources of inspiration for the ideas contained in this book. We want to especially recognize Syed Fazl-Qadir and Anwar Hussain of Pakistan, Kapoor Ahlawat of Jordan, Sagrario Lopez and Maria del Carmen Soto of Honduras, Minister of Education Cecilia de Cano of El Salvador, Minister of Education Nicanor Duarte of Paraguay, Jose Luis Guzman and Hector Lopez of El Salvador, and Vicente Sarubbi and Jesus Montero of Paraguay, for their trust and for the challenges we embarked upon together.

Closer to our institutional home we are in debt to all the institutional and individual associates of the BRIDGES project, too many to mention. We recognize our colleagues at the Harvard Institute for International Development (HIID) with whom we spent many years working together to try to help governments define better education policies. Their friendship and colleagueship created the learning environment that enabled us to explore new ideas and to reflect about our practice. We thank the following friends: the late Russell Davis, Donald Warwick, Thomas Cassidy, Ernesto Cuadra, William Cummings, Abby Riddell, Shirley Burchfield, and Thomas Welsh. Armando Loera and Ernesto Schiéfelbein, with whom we worked closely as they consulted for the project, were also stimulating companions in some of the adventures narrated and analyzed in this book.

Our administrative colleagues at HIID helped us manage the projects that inspired our thinking about the subjects discussed in this book, We thank Claire Brown, Louisa French, Rosanne Kumins, Vicky De Marinis, Richard Pagett, Nino Rosado, Ellen Seidensticker, and Lisa Toste. We are especially grateful to Zoya Omartian and to Sue Rarus, our administrative assistants, for all their good work and help.

Our good friend and colleague Carol Weiss, at the Harvard Graduate School of Education, inspired us with her pioneering scholarship in the sociology of knowledge utilization. Our conversations with Carol helped us refine our own thinking about the subjects developed in this book. Our students at the Harvard Graduate School of Education also encouraged us to clarify ideas and to improve their presentation. Magdalena Rivarola, Claudia Uribe, and Emiliana Vegas read and commented on sections of this book at different times over the past two years.

We are also grateful to our colleague at HIID, Richard Mallon, who provided careful feedback to a draft of the book and to our director, Dwight Perkins, for his broad understanding of development and for the support and respect we received from him that created an environment of academic freedom to investigate the questions we deemed important.

We are also most appreciative of the good works of John Harney, Book Consultants of Boston; James Sabin, Executive Vice President of Greenwood; and of the efforts of Penny Sippel and John Beck, who worked on the production of the book.

Finally, this book owes much of its existence to the support and encouragement of our wives. That we could complete this book at a time of several transitions in our lives is a credit to our wives' ability to take on more than their share to contribute to our sustenance. For this reason and because they have helped us learn about dialogue, a core theme of this text, we have dedicated the book to them.

Introduction

It is now common to argue that we live in a knowledge society in which the utilization of research-based information for decision making is normal (Bohme and Stehr, 1986; Drucker, 1993). Whether that information is produced in scientific laboratories or is produced through action (Gibbons, Limojes, Nowatney, Schwartzmann, Scott, and Trow, 1995), knowledge utilization, and specifically the utilization of research-based knowledge or research utilization, is claimed to be common, or at least highly desirable. The utilization of research-based knowledge promises greater success in achieving objectives for a just and prosperous society (Toffler, 1990).

Research to inform decisions about education has been expanding rapidly for at least forty years. Research and analysis were used first as a means to support educational planning. Recently, these activities have fallen under the title of policy analysis. The growth is most visible in rich countries but just as dramatic in poor countries where scarce resources have been invested in research activities with the hope that they will result in better education and development.

Enthusiasm for research and research utilization in policy making has been tempered in recent years. Questions about the returns to research utilization occurred first for the physical sciences (Snow, 1959) and recently for the social sciences and education (Havelock, 1972; Weiss, 1977). The concerns have been motivated by evidence that the massive production of research information has not generated significant changes in patterns of decision making. The quality of policy choices that have been made is not commensurate with the volume of research findings available. Studies on knowledge utilization (Feldman, 1989) document the difficulties that researchers experience in getting policy makers to make use of their findings.

Our personal experience is testimony to that difficulty. We started as researchers, eager to help struggling countries improve their education systems. We were convinced that our skills in designing research and analyzing data would make an important difference. To our great dismay and chagrin, we found it difficult to get decision makers to listen to us. When they did listen, they often were critical of what we had to say and seldom followed our advice, it seemed.

Our epiphany followed an event in Pakistan when we made our first public report of findings and analysis based on the most comprehensive education research ever done in that country. We were confident of our data, and we spent three days preparing our presentation. Most of our concern was how to explain our complicated statistical procedures to an audience with no background in statistics or research. We met with the top education administrators for all four provinces of Pakistan—a blue-ribbon group. They gave us the floor the first day, and we presented our findings, complete with transparencies and handouts. The next day they made presentations in response to what they had heard. Almost all their comments were negative, denying the validity and usefulness of our reports. On the third day they drew up recommendations for action, many of which directly contradicted what we had recommended.

Stunned and a bit embarrassed by this experience, we have since focused our careers on learning how to use our skills in ways that can be appreciated by the audiences we seek to serve. We have been fortunate in that our audiences have been patient and willing to teach us. Even the Pakistani officials who were critical were willing to give us a second audience. The same facts were on the table in the second meeting, but with a different strategy. The results were much more positive.

This book is about our understanding of how the process of deciding about education, or education policy making, can be informed by research-based knowledge. The model we propose at the end of the book is based on our personal knowledge gained through experience. Perhaps it will seem commonsensical. Our learning, however, has not been easy, as demonstrated by the cases that report our mistakes, presented in Chapter 7 through Chapter 12. Much of what we now understand contradicts what we learned when we were first trained in research. We still meet policy advisors whose ap-

proaches are like those that we used to follow and have now abandoned because the approaches do not work.

The book is divided into four parts. Part I introduces basic concepts and discusses why it is so difficult to use research findings in
policy making. Part II describes a variety of approaches that have
been followed. We have organized these as ranging from methods
of dissemination to methods of dialogue. Part III presents six case
studies of research utilization in educational policy making. These,
too, are arranged from a dissemination to a dialogic approach. Part
IV presents our model of how to inform policy with research-based
knowledge. As personal knowledge, our understandings stand as
untested hypotheses. We are actively working to test them and invite others to do the same.

Concepts and Issues

Part I is an attempt to clarify the central issues caught up in the problem of knowledge utilization. We begin in Chapter 1 with a discussion of why research utilization is important, that is, why more use should be made of research-based knowledge. The issue is clear: Education could be better than it is now, and we know how to go about making it better. In other words, we believe that some people do know how to make education better. The difficulty is that that knowledge is not widely shared. Many decisions about education policy are made without access to or use of research-based knowledge. Chapter 1 presents several examples taken from our experience. The importance of using research is increasing as the context in which education systems operate changes as a result of the forces called globalization. Policy making that ignores scientific understanding of this context dooms education systems to irrelevance.

Chapter 1 attempts to explain why there is so little utilization of research in education policy making. In part, this is a function of the ways in which researchers and policy makers have approached the questions of knowledge and policy up until now. Chapter 1 reviews these various approaches and suggests the type of research that has been shown to be most useful for policy. The question then becomes, How should that research be conducted?

Chapter 2 takes up the other half of the problem: policy making. We believe that part of the problem of knowledge utilization is how policy has been conceptualized. We suggest an alternative defini- tion which denies the dualism of research and policy. We continue the discussion in Chapter 3, which deals with the various actors involved in the policy making process. Much of the work on plan- ning and policy analysis appears to assume that only professional educators and perhaps government officials are involved in the pro- cess. We distinguish between the announcement of policy and its actual formulation and suggest that the list of possible actors is quite large. Who gets involved varies from issue to issue, and who is involved at any moment is a function of stages in the process. As a consequence, knowledge utilization can be common among some actors in the policy process and unknown among others. This makes the process of informing policies in education complex.

Chapter 1

Research Utilization: Why It Is Important, Why It Is an Issue, Why It Is Difficult

We once were invited to Egypt as consultants when Egypt was facing a serious problem of access to schooling. Many schools had been forced to shorten class hours and use buildings for two groups of students. On the other hand, there were classrooms in the villages with less than ten students. Even after all local children had been enrolled, there were not enough students to justify the number of first grade classes that had been required in previous years and some classes were standing empty.

This was a new issue for Egypt. Perhaps it never would have been a problem except that parents in one of the towns with double-shift schools complained to an enterprising newspaper reporter while the country was in the middle of its first free elections in a number of years. The minister of education, a candidate for office, was eager to insure that this did not happen again.

As long as anyone could remember, classrooms had been built by looking at enrollments from the previous year. Each school sent enrollment data to the central Ministry of Education where they were tabulated and sent to the Planning Department. Actually, we found out that the enrollment figures were always two years old, as it took that long for the data to be processed. The Planning Office had limited capacity for computation and therefore aggregated data from individual schools to the level of districts. Almost all districts

included both rural and urban schools. No one had complained
before; the traditional way of estimating classroom requirements
worked well enough. However, now the country was beginning to
industrialize, and employment opportunities in cities and towns
were drawing many families out of rural areas. Migration was selec-
tive; some regions of the country were experiencing high rates of
urbanization while others were not growing at all. Planners in the
central ministry had no awareness of the population shifts.

This was a relatively easy problem to solve. Even without the aid
of computers it was possible to organize enrollment data at the level
of schools to provide much more sensitive forecasts of changes in
the number of children who would be seeking enrollment. Within a
year the proportion of empty and overcrowded classrooms was
sharply reduced. A year later the minister invited us back to help
with other problems.

In a stable, unchanging world, decisions that worked before can
be made again without understanding of why they work. However,
in a changing world, tradition no longer provides security. Choices
have to be made with respect to which objectives to pursue in what
sequence, the combinations of physical and financial resources that
are required and the people to use and manage those resources,
how long the effort should be made, and how to tell when the effort
is failing and should be corrected or has succeeded and can be ter-
minated. These decisions are most likely to be correct and result in
the desired outcomes when they are based on a correct and comprehensive understanding of the current and possible future situations and of the organization itself.

A DEFINITION OF RESEARCH

The problem in Egypt was solved with the help of research. *Research* and related concepts of *information* and *data* can be used
for a variety of meanings. For example, Chapman and Mahlck (1993)
use *data* and *information* as synonyms sometimes and as cause and
effect other times. To avoid confusion, we understand research to
mean the following: (1) actions by persons that involve the compi-
lation or organization of observable facts or data; (2) the arrangement of the data using analytic or synthetic techniques; and (3) the
ability to explain or interpret the data in terms of non-observed concepts or constructs. We use *research* as a synonym with *policy analysis*, in which the objective is to define problems and identify effective
solutions for them.

The results of research or policy analysis are different from those
of other activities that involve data. All management processes use

data of some kind even if they do not use the results of research. Welsh (1993) notes that all organizations have rumor mills, insider information, leaks, and moles that testify to the importance of data in management. But these kinds of data are not generated using the *scientific method*, a set of procedures that maximizes the likelihood that independent observers will report the same data and which provides a means for testing the usefulness of the explanations of the data. The mere collection and reporting of education statistics is not research, although those actions might be a part of a research process.

Research is the term commonly applied to systematic methods to collect and analyze information for the purpose of generating understanding. We use *research utilization* to refer to the systematic efforts made by decision makers to collect information about their situation and to use that information in deciding upon a course of action. The most complete research not only collects and analyzes data to describe a situation but constructs an explanation or provides an understanding of the situation. Research utilization not only helps decision makers choose courses of action but helps them identify what their choices are. Part of our assignment in Egypt was to help ministry officials understand their options. The simple research we did together was sufficient for the problem at hand. However, as change continued in Egypt, new demands were made on the education system. Traditional solutions no longer worked. The ministry had to develop a new understanding of what was possible and how to achieve it.

Of course, what is at stake is much more than just the location of a few schools. Education is the largest industry in every country of the world. The decisions made affect the lives of many children, spend millions of dollars, and can have long-term consequences for the country's economic growth and political stability. Yet, in country after country, decisions are made on the basis of what was done before or on ill-founded guesses or myths about how schools operate and how children learn.

WHY THERE SHOULD BE MORE
RESEARCH UTILIZATION

There are three major arguments to explain why most countries should dramatically increase utilization of research in education. The first is that even though the environments in which they have been operating may have been relatively unchanging, education systems achieve much less than they could and expend more valuable resources than is necessary for what they do achieve. The second is that the problem is not so much a shortage of research as it is a lack of utilization. In all the countries in which we have worked, research reports pile up in university libraries and sometimes even on ministry shelves but are seldom read. Decisions are made without consulting research already done and without doing any additional research. The third is that our world is changing rapidly, requiring new efforts to understand how education can be organized in order to contribute to economic and social objectives.

Education Could Be Much More Effective and Efficient Than It Is

Research on education has a long history, but the history of policy research on education might be dated as beginning in 1966 with the publication of the Coleman Report. This was the first national study of determinants of student achievement at the level of schools. It was the first comprehensive effort to identify those factors that explain why some children have high scores on tests of curriculum knowledge and others do not. Prior to 1967, research sought to explain why individual students learned. The Coleman Report, the Plowden study in Great Britain, and a number of other studies in developed and developing countries took up the issue of why some schools were more effective than others.

Since 1967 we have developed a more or less coherent model of how schooling works and the major factors that contribute to its effectiveness. The model seeks to explain variations in levels of students' learning of curriculum material as a function of what happens in schools. The central variables are *time on task* and the *learning rate* of students. *Time on task* refers to the amount of time students spend engaged in trying to learn curriculum content. The *learning rate* is how much of that content a particular student can learn in a given unit of time. The model specifies the factors that increase time on task and student learning rate that are influenced by what takes place in schools, or what is subject to school-based policies.

Opportunity to learn is another term for describing the importance of time on task. Research shows clearly that policies that increase the exposure that students have to the curriculum increase levels of learning. Exposure to curriculum can take place inside and outside of school. For example, policies that encourage time spent doing homework which exposes students to the curriculum are related to higher levels of learning.

The major policy blocks are those affecting teacher characteristics, teacher and student behavior in classrooms, instructional materials, and organizational factors that affect time allocation to curriculum study. There are important gaps in our understanding of how to translate this model into practice.

Over the past twenty-eight years, research has contributed to identifying for policy makers the singular importance of the teacher as a determinant of amount of student learning. More than curriculum or instructional materials, the teacher is the central actor. But we have not yet cracked the puzzle of how best to prepare teachers for their important task. For example, research on teacher characteristics has not yet identified criteria that would be useful in teacher selection except that teachers with high levels of academic knowledge or general intelligence are more effective teachers. We still do not know how to train teachers to insure that they will be effective.

This lack of understanding is especially striking given that we have at least two centuries of experience in training teachers and thousands and thousands of studies describing what a good teacher is like. How is it that the practical knowledge embedded in the experience of thousands of teacher trainers and supervisors has not been converted into policy research and policies that are effective?

Over time, research has helped policy makers shift from a conception of teachers as deliverers of curriculum packages to a conception of teachers as managers of the learning process that takes place in the classroom. Central in this management is the allocation of the scarce resource of time. The most successful teachers in terms of student learning outcomes are those who keep their children attending to the learning task. Often, this requires responding differentially to children. We have come to understand that a major advantage of private schools over public schools is that through selection they can reduce student heterogeneity which reduces the demand on the teacher to respond differentially to students.

Some public school systems have attempted to achieve the same outcome by streaming or tracking students by dividing them into separate classes on the basis of intellectual ability. This kind of differentiation is, of course, what most characterizes the factory school which standardizes inputs and outputs in order to increase efficiency and total product. Researchers have shown but have not yet been able to persuade policy makers that this kind of policy results in different amounts of inputs to students in the different tracks. In general, students from low income families populate the slower tracks, and they receive the least prepared teachers and fewer materials. Also, according to research, the tracking system encourages teachers to lower their expectations for student learning. Students are aware of what is demanded of them. When expectations are lower, they spend less time trying to learn.

Research has also shown that instructional materials can be designed to substitute for teachers, especially for teachers who have low classroom management skills. Highly scripted instructional materials that tell teachers and students what to do take the place of formal instruction by the teacher. Students can work on these materials at their own pace, overcoming the problem of classroom heterogeneity and freeing the teacher to work on maintaining high levels of expectations for every student. These materials have been tested successfully in a number of systems in Africa and Asia and are the center instrument of the Escuela Nueva of rural Colombia. But policy makers are not yet persuaded of their efficacy, do not believe claims made on their behalf, or do not understand how to reorganize their systems in order to use this approach.

In general, research on school and classroom organization has had the least effect on education policies. The only research that has had any significant effect on policy is research on class size. Many policy makers are now persuaded that they can allow class sizes to grow without having any significant effect on levels of student learning. Research showing that students can learn as much in multigraded classrooms and in double-shift schools has generally been ignored. The reorganization of governance through decentralization was motivated primarily by political considerations and not informed by research. Only now is research available that suggests what can and cannot be accomplished by shifting authority for education policy toward schools.

The development of a general model of schooling has made it possible to understand the importance of contextual factors in selecting policies. The definition of a model specified the boundaries of our understanding but did not deny that this model operates as part of a larger system. The structure of the larger system and the key factors within it have not yet been mapped. Many of them are better known by the policy makers than by the researchers, as they reflect actions that researchers seldom see or are allowed to see. It is commonplace to call these political factors but too often that is an excuse for not studying and understanding them. Communication between policy makers and researchers will be required to reach an understanding of these factors.

We now have a general model of how schooling produces student learning and an enormous volume of research to illustrate the model's claims. The model is still primarily the intellectual property of researchers. It could be said that we know how to make schools more effective and more efficient. The question is whether the *we* that knows are those who make decisions.

Research Utilization Is Scarce in Policy Making

In spite of the long history and all the knowledge accumulated through research many education policies are not based in research or technical analysis. Education researchers generally think that much more is known about how to expand educational opportunity than is used to make policy choices.

The behavior of education organizations when they go about their business as usual or when they try to change suggests that there is limited consideration of the knowledge accumulated through efforts of rational inquiry about the options which are most effective in helping students learn. Upon close examination, many efforts to increase educational opportunity through changing curricula, training teachers, improving supervision, or reorganizing schools are better characterized as tinkering with the elements of the system than as the results of informed decision making. In part, this stems from what it means to decide in an education system and from how research-based knowledge is accumulated and processed, two points that we will come back to later.

Examples of Poor Use of Research to Design and Implement Education Policy. An example of the type of tinkering which illustrates many education reforms is seen in various attempts to implement change across the world. We present three examples of efforts to change the content of education and one case in which an attempt was made to change educational management.

Knowledge gained through research consistently points out the need for mutual reinforcement between changes in instructional technology and changes in opportunities for professional development of teachers (Darling-Hammond and McLaughlin, 1995). Most people familiar with the research literature on curriculum reform would agree that the curriculum comes alive in the classroom as a result of the choices made by teachers as to how to use instructional time. For a curriculum reform to be successful, teachers must be trained in new instructional practices.

This appears obvious, but across decades and across countries as far apart as Pakistan, Venezuela, and Paraguay, policy makers have attempted to change curriculum and instruction without attending to teachers.

In Pakistan in the early 1970s the Ministry of Education spent several years designing an innovation to improve quality in primary schools. They came up with a teaching kit which included about one hundred items, such as beakers, a national flag, an abacus, and other materials. Sixty thousand kits were produced and delivered. The kits were based on the use of a pedagogy that stimulated student participation in small groups and student learning from direct experiences rather than the use of the traditional pedagogy based on rote memorization. The traditional pedagogy is what was taught in teacher training colleges. The hope was that teachers would adopt the new pedagogy for most of their instruction.

Sadly, this did not happen. In a survey of primary schools across Pakistan we found that few of the teachers (about one in five) used the teaching kit more than seven times a year. The rate of use was so low that the teaching kits and their use had no impact on student achievement in mathematics and science. Only 22 percent of the teachers had received any training on the teaching kit and most teachers and administrators did not understand the purpose of or need for the kit (Warwick, Reimers, and McGinn, 1992).

This particular innovation had been designed by an international agency and transported to Pakistan. Perhaps it had worked in some other setting in which conditions were more appropriate. We know today that the designers should have taken into account research which demonstrates that teachers are the most critical factor in curriculum reform. We know that reforms which attempt to be teacher proof have a bad record.

The 1980 education reform in Venezuela also ignored research on the importance of training teachers to change the curriculum. In this case a new education law was passed which extended basic education from six to nine years. New curricula were designed, aimed at developing higher-level cognitive processes. A decade later the reform was pronounced a failure. Venezuelan fourteen-year-olds had some of the lowest scores in an international study of reading achievement covering thirty countries (Elley, 1992).

How could an education reform which aimed at helping students to think better end up producing students who could not read? An assessment of teacher education programs found that the reform had essentially ignored teacher training (Villegas-Reimers, 1994). The reformers had passed a new law and produced new curricula and new textbooks but had left teacher training institutions unaltered six years after the initiation of the reform.

In 1992, the government of Paraguay decided to change the curriculum of primary education. New programs were designed with a greater focus on processes of cognitive development. New textbooks were produced reflecting those programs. This time the textbooks were given to the teachers along with training. Training sessions were organized by calling hundreds of teachers from the same grade in nearby schools into a nine-day orientation. During this orientation the new curriculum was introduced and the programs and textbooks were delivered. The teachers returned to their schools. Because the training was organized one grade each year, that is, first grade in 1993, second grade in 1994, and so forth, the teachers had no one else to discuss the new curriculum with when they returned to school.

In a series of evaluations conducted in 1995 when one of us was the resident advisor to the Ministry of Education of Paraguay, we found out that teachers rejected this form of training. They said it barely provided them with the motivation to attempt to teach differently. They said it left them to their own resources in a school where no one else shared their enthusiasm and left them without further opportunities to continue developing skills. This approach to training ignored research-based knowledge on teacher education which suggests that teachers, as adults, learn better when they can integrate the new knowledge with prior knowledge and experience. Training is more successful when it is locally based and provides opportunities for iterations between assimilation of new concepts and practice (Shulman, 1990).

The last case we present to illustrate that decisions are rarely based in research-based knowledge refers to an effort of the Ministry of Education in El Salvador to change school organization and management.

In 1991, the Ministry of Education of El Salvador launched an ambitious program to promote community participation in school management which essentially ignored the existing research-based knowledge on decentralization of the subject. Five years later the program had expanded and was the main policy initiative of the ministry. Local evaluations of the program which pointed to correctable flaws were ignored.

There is an old tradition of research that asks whether highly centralized educational administration is the reason behind much of the ineffectiveness, inefficiency, and inequity of education systems. An extensive body of literature documents this long strand of research on decentralization (Clune, 1993; Davies, 1990; Lauglo, 1995; Hannaway and Carnoy, 1993). The early research on decentralization was simplistic and confusing in that it focused on vaguely defined concepts of centralization and decentralization. More recent studies define the functions (curriculum, personnel, finance, and construction) and levels (national, regional, local, or school) that might be decentralized. Another strand of the literature has further refined the options by distinguishing between decentralization, deconcentration, delegation, and devolution.

An important conclusion of the research is that transferring functions to decentralized levels other than the school does not necessarily improve (or decrease) the quality of the services provided, in part because it does not automatically lead to changes in the organization of the school, and therefore does not lead to changes in the teaching process (Fuhrman and Johnson, 1994; McGinn and Street, 1986; Kannapel, Moore, Coe, and Aagaard, 1995; Prawda, 1992; Walberg and Niemiec, 1994). Decentralized units may inhibit school autonomy as much as, or more than, centralized ones.

A recent strand of this research examines efforts to empower school communities (Wong, 1993). The school-based management literature proposes that the effectiveness of school organization can be increased by increasing the power of parents and teachers. This literature addresses the following question: How can public schools be made more responsive to local conditions and accountable to local communities? The literature on school-based management lacks a definitive evaluation of the impacts of this approach on quality (Malen, Ogawa, and Kranz, 1990). Research on the impact of school-based management on parent participation suggests that "school professionals almost always become the key decision-makers in decentralized governance" (Wong, 1993, 592).

The existing stock of knowledge on this subject suggests that the strong pressures in favor of decentralization during the 1970s and 1980s were inspired more by hopes and ideology than by rigorous inquiry and analysis. There was little research utilization in early policies of decentralization. The lesson that decentralization does not necessarily improve quality or equity has been learned over twenty years of experience at a high cost. School autonomy and community participation could turn out to be just a new fad. Further up-front reflection and critical evaluation are needed to reduce some of the costs and the time required to learn some lessons.

One of the lessons learned from the research on decentralization is that it is important to elaborate an operational definition of which functions are to involve local levels. Knowledge on this subject was advanced significantly only when vague notions of decentralization were replaced by specific references to the functions that would be carried out by different levels, such as definition of goals, identification of policies, teacher selection, curriculum design, supervision, financing, and so forth.

Most of these lessons learned from earlier research on decentralization and school-based management were ignored when the Ministry of Education of El Salvador decided to launch the education with participation of the community (EDUCO) program in 1991.

The promoters of the program acknowledge that the idea to adopt this national policy was based on local experience and that there was little consideration of knowledge gained elsewhere. Furthermore, local evaluations of the program suggesting that it had no impact in student achievement or local participation have had modest impact on further decisions to expand it.

During the twelve-year civil war which ended in 1989, many local communities began to hire their own teachers in response to the frequent closure of schools during the war. The ministry estimates that in 1988 there were about 1,000 community groups which contributed more than $13 million, or 10 percent of the education budget.

EDUCO began in May 1991 as an approach to expand access to preschool education and the first cycle of primary education in rural areas. This cycle consists of the first three grades of primary school. In the first year of the program, six experimental projects were established (three sections of preschool and three of first grade) in rural areas in three departments of El Salvador. Parents in each one of the six schools in the community were organized into Community Associations for Basic Education (ACEs). The ACEs are entities with legal recognition. Therefore, they can receive funds from the government in exchange for the provision of services. The ministry provides each ACE with enough funds to hire a teacher and to buy limited school supplies. The role of the ministry is to help organize the ACEs and to train teachers and supervise their performance. The ministry has also established the criteria for teacher selection: All teachers in EDUCO must be college graduates. A unit was established in the Ministry of Education to coordinate the project.

The objectives of this first phase of experimentation were to design and test the procedures of the program and all training materials. In July 1991 the program began a phase of expansion to other localities in the same three departments. Ninety-six classrooms of preschool and 141 of first grade were established. In 1992 the program was extended to all fourteen departments of the country. In 1993 the Ministry of Education began a phase of generalizing the innovation, expanding coverage in all fourteen departments.

The number of community associations increased rapidly from 237 in 1991 to 958 in 1992. The number of classrooms opened under the program increased from 263 to 1,126 in the same period, and the number of students from 10,520 to 45,040. In 1993, 10 percent of rural students in grades one to three were enrolled in EDUCO.

In EDUCO the ACEs hire teachers with one-year renewable contracts, and they pay the teacher and manage the small fund for school supplies. Community associations in turn have one-year renewable contracts with the Ministry of Education. Community associations are managed by an elected committee which includes members of the community but are comprised primarily of parents of students enrolled in the school.

There are questions about the consolidation of EDUCO because of the fast expansion. Several educators in El Salvador consider that the experience needs to mature and deepen, developing the role of the community associations so they can effectively influence delivery of high-quality education by the teachers.

The program has faced opposition, particularly from teacher unions and from leaders in the zones formerly in conflict, where it is perceived as a strategy of political co-optation. In many of the areas formerly in conflict, an alternative form of teaching emerged during the war—the popular teachers (*maestros populares*). These were members of the community who were given responsibility to teach after the official teachers had fled these areas. The political opposition provided some organization and support to these popular teachers. In 1995 a joint verification done by the Ministry of Education and the Coordinating Group of these teachers in the opposition documented that the popular teachers were providing education to some 17,000 students in rural areas. Some in the opposition see EDUCO as a strategy of the central state to neutralize a loosely organized network of popular teachers who identified with the opposition during the war. EDUCO has been established disproportionately in the eastern part of the country in the areas that had been in conflict in spite of the fact that there are higher percentages of children of school age out of school in the western part of the country. Teacher unions also opposed being hired by community associations, which fragmented the relationship of the trade union with a single employer—the ministry (Reimers, 1997b).

The evaluations conducted by the Ministry of Education and by the World Bank, which funded the program, consistently point out that while access has improved, results regarding community participation are mixed and that there are no appreciable gains in student achievement. While community associations have successfully managed the responsibilities delegated to them by the ministry, such as receiving funds and hiring teachers, it is less clear that their participation has had a significant impact on school organization and management. An independent assessment of the education sector conducted by the Harvard Institute for International Development (HIID) in 1993 compared a sample of 140 EDUCO and traditional rural schools. No differences were found in teacher absenteeism, teaching practices, instructional time, or community participation (Reimers, 1995). When faced with these findings, Ministry of Education officials responsible for the program went to great pains to question the validity of the results and showed no inclination to question the rationale of the project. They did this in spite of the fact that these results were consistent with findings from another survey reported in a World Bank study of the project. That study found no major differences in school or teacher characteristics or student attendance. There are no statistically significant differences in teacher absences or instructional time (World Bank, 1994).

Findings from the World Bank and HIID studies suggested that the project did not have the expected effects in teacher attendance or in providing students with opportunities to learn. The same could have anticipated examining existing research-based knowledge which pointed out the loosely developed theory concerning how management changes translated into changes in pedagogical conditions which influenced how children learned in classrooms. Furthermore, the design of EDUCO missed opportunities to develop a program theory informed by the stock of available knowledge, clearly specifying how the proposed changes in school management were expected to change supply and demand factors which influence how children learn.

How common are these experiences? Are these four cases anomalies in how decisions are made to change education systems? On the contrary, we think they illustrate how education change generally is designed and implemented. Examples of how research-based knowledge is used to inform education policy choices are hard to find.

A 1982 symposium that discussed the research and policy relationship primarily in Europe and in the United States concluded the following: (Husen and Kogan, 1984)

The evidence is patchy and inconclusive on the actual impacts. Diffusion and enlightenment are the dominant metaphors rather than impact or cause and effect. (1984, 69) . . . The relationship is much more diffuse and hard to pinpoint than had been hitherto conceived. Scholarship contributes by putting certain issues on the agenda of public debate and by inspiring demands for political action. Research, particularly through critical analysis, often generates ideas more than specific facts or knowledge. It contributes to reinterpreting an issue by drawing attention to aspects that have gone unnoticed. It might affect the belief systems of the general public. It can contribute to achieving consensus about an issue. Political decisions are made within a context of accommodation. The decision is not clear cut but is an attempt to arrive at resolutions that can accommodate a maximum of interests represented by groups and individuals who want to influence the decision or policy-making process. (p. 74)

The World Is Changing: New Problems
Require New Understandings

Globalization is no longer a stranger and is discussed daily on radio and television, in newspapers and magazines, and in board meetings and faculty meetings. The changes we attribute to globalization are accompanied by changes in all aspects of our lives.

Globalization is a complex set of flows or movements that include the following:

1. People moving within and across national boundaries as workers, refugees, and tourists. These people bear but are not the sole source of information.
2. Information, understood as data in the form of scientific reports, news broadcasts, statistics, and documentary films and videos. The flow of information is greatly facilitated by the spread of new technologies.
3. New technologies of communication and of production and distribution which permit radical changes in the organization and standard of life and the distribution of wealth. New technologies also permit an incredible flow of financial resources.
4. Financial resources, available in daily volumes that exceed the total annual product of most countries of the world and which are beyond the control of any government. Facilitated by new technologies, but associated with tourism and capital flows, there is also a great movement across cultural boundaries of images and ideas.
5. Images and ideas carried in television programs, videos and films, music, books and magazines, and, of course, conversations and formal speeches (Appadurai, 1990; Deutsch, 1966; Gellner, 1983).

The content and volume of these flows affect not only what we learn but also how we learn and how we apply what we learn. That latter is essential, as the stock and flow of information available in the world, including that from research, will increase dramatically in the future.

Among other effects, the flows contribute to changes in the following:

1. The state that has been in all but a few countries the patron and main builder and shaper of education at all levels.
2. The economic return and political and intellectual attractiveness of different technologies of production and distribution.
3. The kinds of knowledge, skills, and values required by, and most likely to survive and prosper in, a new social order. All these require dramatic changes in how education is organized.

Changes in the composition and strength of the state are already affecting education systems, especially public education systems, around the world. In many countries of the world, governments are less able to raise the funds required to finance expanding demand for education. Governments are under pressure from both national and transnational sources to devolve power to smaller units of governance, to decentralize education, and to permit the participation of actors that previously had no voice in the decision making. In some instances, international assistance agencies and transnational corporations have significant influence over decisions; in even more cases, private interests have increasing involvement in deciding about the allocation and disbursement of public funds.

Changes in technology affect not only how it is possible to teach but what should be taught. Changes in technologies of instruction are linked with changes in technologies of production; method and content influence each other. For the most part, public education systems in the world were organized at the end of the eighteenth century to match the new technology of production associated with manufacture and the assembly-line factory. In the twentieth century this technology of production has spread around the world and is the dominant method of organizing human activity (Oman, 1994).

Under the factory model, schools were organized to permit mass education, requiring standardization of inputs (selection and training of teachers, design of classrooms, production of textbooks, and uniform curriculum). The effects were dramatic. Where this organization was attempted, schooling mushroomed, fostered by and contributing to rapid industrialization and economic growth.

Today, increased global competition and consequent risk has encouraged some firms in Japan and other Asian countries, and more recently in the United States and Europe, to abandon the factory production technology in favor of a flexible production technology. The key differences between the two technologies of production are as follows: (Oman, 1994)

1. Factory production generated increases in productivity by capturing the knowledge of highly-skilled crafts workers and converting it to rule-driven, routine production processes controlled by management (Braverman, 1974). Flexible production reintegrates thinking and doing, giving workers participation in the production process under management control. The effects are further improvements in productivity (Womack, Jones, and Roos, 1990).

2. The process of reintegration of thinking and doing can take place in all sectors of the firm, from design of the product to marketing and distribution. Integration of these various elements of the firm makes it possible to bring designers and producers together with clients. This shortens time to production and time to market which reduces the need for large inventories and increased sales. The term *just-in-time production* is applied to this aspect.

3. All members of the firm participate in the pursuit of high levels of quality. Decision making is carried out in groups (sometimes called quality circles) which are given control over the production process in return for responsibility for meeting objectives. Workers no longer are specialized but instead require a broad range of skills. Training is continuous and often collective. Wages are linked with group rather than individual performance.

4. Production sites are often smaller using flexible production as compared to assembly-line factory production. Plants are located closer to
   suppliers to reduce time to deliver inputs and closer to markets to reduce time to deliver finished goods. The integrated design–production–
   marketing system increases variety in products by permitting smaller
   runs, or volume of production.

5. Central to the management of flexible production is the availability of
   information about all aspects of the process at all times. This information has to be widely circulated across levels and divisions to insure
   coordination. The requirement for information requires that plants be
   located close to consumers. The effect on transnational firms is called
   global localization. Transmission of information within firms is facilitated by emphasis on interpersonal relations, corporation culture, and
   training in communication skills.

Not all production will ever be carried out using flexible production
methods, any more than the assembly line was ever the most common method of organization of work. Why, then, should we expect
that a general shift toward the new technology of production will
have any impact on the content and organization of education? In
general, education was very much affected by the shift away from
crafts production toward management-controlled factories. The new
shift in technology of production is of the same magnitude and therefore likely to have an impact of equivalent size on education.

Factory industrialization served as a powerful metaphor for the
organization of all society, including schools and universities. The
metaphor promoted standardization across institutions (accredita-
tion systems), disaggregation of the production process into small
parts (credit hours), sharp divisions between disciplines pursuing
the same truth, and centralization leading to massive institutions
in which bureaucratization became the only possible management
technology. The collegium was transformed into a vast collection
of shops producing parts of knowledge which somehow were to be
assembled by learners and society into a meaningful whole.

The metaphors implied by concepts such as flexible production,
quality circles, and total quality management place more emphasis
on groups than on individuals as the agents of production. Schools
and universities organized according to these metaphors will still
have to give students a grounding in the concepts and facts of the
disciplines, but much more attention will be given to teaching methods of learning. More use will be made of self-instruction as the
preferred method for learning basic concepts and facts. Teachers
will provide directions to bodies of knowledge but will place greater
emphasis on applications. Students will spend relatively less time
on fact acquisition and more time on experiential learning. Greater

emphasis will be given to learning at the work site, whether it be a factory or hospital or courtroom or boardroom (Ojeda Delgado, 1994).

Group learning will be privileged over individual learning. Emphasis will be placed more on the diversity of perspectives that can be brought to solve problems than on identification of a single correct or best approach. Noncognitive methods of expression will be encouraged to stimulate creativity in the solution of messy problems and to facilitate communication. This will require changes in student assessment procedures and in the direction of portfolio and performance assessment. Attention to applications of knowledge will increase interdisciplinary work. Over time, this will lead to a blurring of disciplinary lines and the creation of new disciplines that are amalgams of present ones.

Teaching will expand to recover methods deemphasized by the adaptation of the factory metaphor of production to the production of learning. These older methods make more use of noncognitive dimensions of human experience. This kind of teaching and learning emphasizes construction of knowledge through action over discovery of existing fact. Purpose defines the value of knowledge, and subjectivity becomes as important as objectivity. Because most problems require group action, intersubjectivity, or the shared understanding of both fact and purpose, is essential.

These metaphors are being seized upon by leaders in developing countries as a means to achieve the levels of income enjoyed by the early industrialized countries. In many cases, without the benefit of research to justify the expectations held, education systems are being reformed to conform to the new emblems of modernity. The impacts on education systems will be profound, and without the guidance of research many impacts may well be disastrous for countries with limited resources.

WHY IS THERE SO LITTLE RESEARCH UTILIZATION IN POLICY FORMULATION?

There are several reasons to explain the poor link between research and policy in education. One set of reasons has to do with what researchers do. Another set of reasons has to do with how policy is designed and implemented. As we have seen it, education change is rarely the result of decisions made by a decision maker highly placed at the top. Policy change is the result of a process of negotiating competing interests within the education organization and with the external environment where the system operates. As discussed in Chapter 2, education decisions are shaped gradually. They evolve over time in iterations between policy definition and implementation. There are rare instances when a decision is made in ways which mark a sharp cut with past practice, and it is in the nature of education change to evolve in a flow of events and practices where the past and the intended future coexist for some time, much as the forward and backward currents meet in a wave. Chapter 3 reviews in greater detail why education policies are so difficult to inform.

Understanding the poor links between education research and policy calls not for an understanding of the mismatches between the products of research and decision making, but for an understanding of how the processes of education research influence the processes of policy design and implementation. Our challenge is to understand the reciprocal influences of two dynamic systems in order to understand the mismatches between the contents of research (research knowledge as a product) and the contents of policy (policy decisions as outcomes).

Husen (1994) has argued that the poor coupling between education research and decision making stems from the differences in the backgrounds of researchers and decision makers, differences in their social values, and differences in institutional settings. Researchers generally work in university settings and obtain credit for research which is recognized by their peers. They investigate problems and present findings in the context of paradigms, theories, and methods which are recognized in their discipline. They place a high premium in their autonomy to reach conclusions about the problems they study. Policy makers have a more practical orientation and a clearer sense of their own degrees of freedom to implement policy. They value research to the extent that it is instrumental in achieving certain policy objectives. These differences characterize the contrasting ethos of researchers and policy makers. Policy makers often judge research findings insufficiently conclusive to support decisions. Methods of research that dismember policy problems into subproblems that can be investigated more easily leave decision makers with bits and pieces of information but no synthesis of problems of concern.

In many countries, much of the education research is produced in universities and is conceived, funded, and carried out in ways that have limited links to potential users and which do not take into account the perspectives of users in drawing the implications of findings. Much of the education research is not very usable by policy makers, even if the mechanisms existed to present the latter group with the products of research.

This characterization of the different ethos of research and policy is consistent with the reasons advanced by Levin (1982) to explain why much research is not useful for policy:

First, it must address the particular questions that are being faced by the policy maker. Second, it must be timely in providing appropriate research findings in time for making the correct decision. Third, it should be written in such a way as to be understandable to a person who is not an expert on educational research. And, fourth, it should not violate the particular political constraints which are placed upon the policy maker. (p. 162)

Some authors have proposed that the expectation that educational research will have immediate policy application is based on unrealistic assumptions. Instead, they argue, the main contribution of education research is to shape, challenge, or change the way policy makers and practitioners think about problems (Shavelson, 1988). A conclusion of the 1982 Sweden Symposium on links between education research and policy making was that political decisions often create the context for educational research results to enter the policy arena (Husen and Kogan, 1984).

In addition to the backgrounds and institutional settings of researchers, other factors which constrain the links with policy include the objectives of research. By design most education research is interested in explaining changes in learning outcomes, or some other valued outcome, as a function of a limited set of conditions. The complexity of factors which influence educational reality, however, is subsumed in factors whose influence is canceled, as expressed in the statement, All other things being equal. As a result, when researchers seek explanations they generally come up with a set of limited relationships between factors. In the real world, all other things are not equal. Policy makers are interested not just in the simplifications which are necessary for academic advancement of knowledge but in looking at a problem from the multiple frames provided by the conditions which have been treated as noise in most research.

HOW TO IMPROVE THE RECIPROCAL INFLUENCE
BETWEEN RESEARCH AND POLICY

Two things are required to increase research utilization: changes in the research itself, and changes in the policy formulation process. This section addresses both of these requirements.

Which Type of Research Is Most Useful for Policy?

The Importance of the Researcher's Objectives. A useful way to think about the fit between the way researchers approach their work and education policy is to think about the objectives of the researcher. Vielle (1981) distinguishes four kinds of research according to their purpose: academic, planning, instrumentation, and action. While all types can be useful to a decision maker or policy maker (Vielle, 1981), it is necessary to keep in mind that each answers a different question.

Academic research is designed to answer the question, Are our systems of explanation (theories, models, and conceptual frameworks) correct? The question is answered by rigorous testing of hypotheses drawn from the conceptual framework.

Planning research answers the question, What are the factors that produce the outcome we are seeking? This kind of research uses statistical analysis to generate patterns of relationships among variables.

Instrumentation research answers the question, How can we construct or organize the factors required to produce the desired outcomes? Repeated trial and error methods are used in the instrumentation process in preparing a new curriculum.

Action research asks, Can we in fact produce the outcomes we desire? This question can only be asked by attempting to produce for the entire system the outcomes that are desired. In the end, the objective of the research is the outcomes themselves rather than the knowledge of how to achieve them.

Academic research can help us understand why the world, the particular piece of reality we are interested in, is the way it is. For example, research by Coleman (1966) on the relative contribution of education- and home-related factors to student learning would fit in this category.

Planning research focuses on the contribution of potential policy levers to improve educational opportunity, for example, identifying the relative cost-effectiveness of alternative forms of teacher training in a particular setting (Tatto, Nielsen, and Cummings, 1991).

Instrumentation research develops products through successive iterations between action and assessment innovations. An example would be the design of a new science curriculum in a process of putting together isolated pieces of knowledge gained from evaluations of prior experience and a broad-based research knowledge.

Action research is more interested in change itself than in understanding change. Rapid assessment techniques, beneficiary surveys, and participatory evaluations would fit in this category. Also, we would include formative evaluation research in this broad category. An example would be successive rounds of evaluations of the EDUCO experiment, which actually influenced program theory and implementation.

This characterization of the various purposes of researchers helps us understand why so much knowledge generated by research is not directly relevant for policy. While most researchers are interested in why things in the world are the way they are, policy makers are interested in the way things could be. In the words of Robert F. Kennedy, "Most men see things as they are and ask 'why'. I dream things that never were and ask 'why not'?"

Not All Research Is Relevant. We subscribe to the view that a large part of research activities should not be asked to be immediately relevant for policy. But if research should not be constrained to fit policy, it follows that policy should not be constrained to follow research. Policy statements have two components, namely, goals and the preferred means to achieve those goals. Research that demonstrates that a particular set of procedures is effective in achieving goal *A* does not dictate that goal *A* should be preferred. It would be inappropriate to expect that research on the determinants of *A*, which showed the predictive power of strategies *X, Y,* and *Z* should be a sufficient basis to inform the desirability of these strategies over other options which might lead to the same or different outcomes.

The question about the fit between research and policy is therefore more pertinent regarding certain types of education research. The more pertinent research is designed to anticipate the consequences of action. This is what we understand as policy research as opposed to research designed to explain why the world is the way it is without describing how it could be made to be different. Much education research is not designed to inform choices and therefore provides an inadequate, or at least insufficient, basis for policy. Descriptive or explanatory research can be generalized only to what is, not to new situations the policy maker wants to create.

The limitations of descriptive and explanatory research for policy are seen in the experience with using research on learning to design teacher training programs. During the last twenty years, research on the determinants of student achievement has tried to sort out the relative influences of various school inputs and processes. Summaries of these production function studies have attempted to establish which are the best predictors. A recent review of studies of the determinants of achievement, for instance, finds that while school libraries, instructional time, homework, and textbooks are significant predictors of student learning in at least 75 percent of the studies, teacher knowledge and teacher experience are only significant predictors in 60 percent and 50 percent of the cases (Fuller and Clarke, 1994). A similar review of studies conducted in Latin America concludes that years of schooling, subject matter knowledge, and experience of the teachers are not related to student achievement in about 50 percent of the cases, and that in-service training is never related (Velez, Schiefelbein, and Valenzuela, 1993).

The research implies that teacher characteristics, such as preparation, knowledge, or experience, can be ignored in efforts to reform education systems. To do so has been shown to be a serious mistake. A more pertinent research question would be, Under what circumstances do teacher-related policies matter? And how can teacher practices be changed to expand opportunities for learning gains? Unless education is restructured at some future point to eliminate teachers, the pertinent question is not whether teachers make a difference, but how their influence can be optimized. Researchers and reviewers of research sometimes get carried away and generalize beyond what the evidence they have examined allows.

Limitations on Conclusion Drawing. The mistaken generalization about teacher characteristics stems in part from the limited range of variability of factors, such as training and experience within a single education system. One reason teacher preparation shows little or no effect is because most teachers are already trained and because there are no substantial variations in the quality of training within a single country. Furthermore, most of these studies have examined a fairly restricted set of learning outcomes, focusing on achievement in a few subjects measured with tests emphasizing content mastery. The results should be interpreted as meaning that the existing options for teacher training have no impact, not that teacher training can be dismissed as an option.

Another difficulty in assessing the relative contribution of teachers' subject matter knowledge, general knowledge, specific skills (verbal or mathematical), or pedagogical knowledge is that those factors are confounded in most analyses; their independent contribution cannot be easily sorted out. Another possible explanation for the mixed results which have been found on the impact of teacher skills and training on student learning is that a number of factors mediate these links. While training may influence teacher behavior, other factors both mediate the influence of teachers' behavior on student learning and influence teachers' and students' behavior.

A proper conclusion, in order to be faithful to the constraints of those studies, is that some studies failed to show the impact of teacher characteristics, practices, and learning on student achievement among students because of limitations in the measures employed. Notice should also be taken that even when efforts are made to overcome these limitations, other school inputs (e.g., class size, school resources, nutrition of children, prior academic experience in school and at home, and so forth) affect the relationship between teachers and achievement. It is possible that teachers cannot do much to compensate for overcrowded and impoverished classrooms, undernourished children, and so on. Our knowledge about these interactions and about threshold effects that kick off these interactions is at best rudimentary.

Improving the links between research and policy requires honest communication where researchers can be free to present the evidence as well as help interpret the limits of those findings.

The Process of Conducting Research for Policy

Supporting decision making with research-based knowledge is a complex undertaking. However, we deny that this complexity prevents the systematic arrangement of conditions to engineer an increase in the impact of research-based knowledge on decision making. As we shift our understanding of policy from notions of decision making to notions of policy formation, research-based knowledge can inform the policy agenda and the conversations among stakeholders which go on as policy is formed.

A fruitful strategy involves identifying the multiple groups (stakeholders) that shape how education policies are formed. To maximize the impact of research on policy formation requires addressing these groups as part of the process of research. Much more is involved than just strategies of dissemination. Each group has to be incorporated into the process of generating research-based knowledge. Chapter 6 discusses why this is necessary and how it can be achieved, and it examines a number of cases that shed light on the opportunities and constraints that emerge in attempting to exert this influence.

There is at least one bias in our review of the cases and in the lessons we draw from them. It is the belief that democratic decision making about education policy is preferable to authoritarian decision making, and that processes that allow public scrutiny of policy decisions are superior to processes which do not. It is through this lens that we view favorably participatory processes and processes that allow organizations to learn. These processes permit dialogue to be informed by research and also permit research to be discussed as part of a broader conversation that brings in information and interests which are a necessary part of policy design. We believe that research-based knowledge is constructed within specific value frameworks and that decisions cannot be based solely on research-based evidence.

Scientific knowledge in itself does not have intrinsic normative authority, nor are research-based judgments value-neutral. Our view of the role of research-based knowledge in policy is consistent with what Jurgen Habermas (1971) has called a pragmatic model, as opposed to a decisionistic model, which assumes that science is value-neutral. The pragmatic model also differs from the technocratic model, which assumes that scientific knowledge has intrinsic normative authority (Habermas, 1971). The pragmatic model suggests interactions of reciprocal influence between politicians and researchers in a democratic society. We seek those circumstances in which the pragmatic model can be used without ignoring that in "more restricted decision-making surroundings the decisionistic or even technocratic models may apply" (Lampinen, 1992, 26).

This value orientation is in conflict with some of the organizing structures of educational decision making in many countries, as is the notion that the rationales for public policy should or could be publicly debated and that the basis of decision making could be open to public scrutiny. In our experience, it is possible even in those circumstances to apply the pragmatic model. We believe that in promoting interactions between the processes of research and policy, explicit attempts need to be made to involve outside government, what some might call civil society or the public, in the process of research and in the policy dialogue surrounding research organizations and individuals. This will produce tensions which will generate a wider range of options for change. The involvement of outside organizations will stimulate processes that will nourish the demand for change and sustain reform efforts. We propose deliberately generating conflict or openly addressing latent conflicts by bringing together people and institutions who do not share a common perspective, value, social class, or exposure to outside influences. Adequate management of this conflict involves shifting to negotiation and public dialogue as a means of policy formation, as opposed to imposing the views of a group of government officials or of technocrats in the rest of society.

This view of education policy as the outcome of negotiation is based on the value we place on democratic processes and on our interest in the actual implementation, and not just declaration, of education policies. The gap between implementation and policy is greater when the voices of key stakeholders have been suppressed in the process of policy design. Implementation is an arena where these voices can be heard (Grindle, 1980). Negotiation of policy and up-front conflict management is an attempt to hear pertinent voices at the outset of policy design.

The aim of the process we propose to support decision making with research-based knowledge is to facilitate a dialogue which allows stakeholders to reach a negotiated but informed dialogue. Research can bring fresh air and new perspectives but it has to be incorporated into a process of communication so that it informs the meanings of this collective construction of education problems and options.

Because a participatory approach is so different from standard practice in policy formation, it is to be expected that it will face resistance; the challenge is to recognize small openings and to stay the course in a process that will sometimes be uphill. We illustrate later that it is possible to design processes of technical analysis to support the quality of education policy decisions and to integrate them into processes of democratic dialogue. This requires recognizing the political nature of planning and identifying the relevant groups with a stake in the outcome of planning (stakeholders). This involves creating spaces for collaboration between ministries of education and other organizations representing civil society, such as nongovernment organizations, universities, or advisory committees.

There are reasonable questions about the merits of a participatory process. One asks if there is a risk in broadening participation to actors who have not had the same opportunities for advanced training in specialized analytic techniques and whether that will reduce the quality of the final product. We contend that the inclusion of multiple perspectives in the analysis enriches the quality of the final product. The techniques available for education policy analysis are not such that they can provide a single answer to the causes of and solutions to education problems. Findings about education problems are limited by the methodologies used to investigate them; by the way in which the phenomena of interest are defined and measured; by the events, moments, or people who are sampled; and by the hypotheses of those who investigate. This does not mean that one should dismiss the importance of rigorous inquiry of educational problems, but it does mean that one should be humble about what such an inquiry can yield. Maybe educational policy analysts and researchers can take inspiration from the impact of chaos theory in physics, which speaks of the infinite complexity of even simple systems and moves our understanding of science as truth to understanding science as a process of discovery of patterns and probabilities.

Educational problems as they are faced by policy makers lack the precision to be found in a systematic study that can prespecify all relevant variables. There are pedagogic, economic, legal, bureaucratic, and other dimensions to the problems faced by decision makers and to the alternatives that can be considered. To bring up highly specialized expertise in rational analysis in order to examine problems and identify solutions is a useful exercise but one that by definition simplifies the dimensions of the problem. Therefore, the consideration of alternatives should take place not within the simplified environment of the analyst but in the real world where concrete persons and groups express these multiple interests.

Some of the real problems faced by policy makers have a complexity that defies easy answers. Policy analysis and strategic planning are therefore as much an exercise of discovery through rational inquiry as they are processes of managing negotiations of competing views on the problem. It is only when experts take the risk of making themselves vulnerable to stakeholders, decision makers, and managers by recognizing that they do not know all the answers, that there may be more than one answer, and that we need other answers to have a dialogue to better understand the problem that it is possible to begin to appreciate the complexity of education issues as decision makers face them. Taking that risk is the only course if one wants to provide advice which is relevant for real life decision making.

The business of education reform exceeds the best intentions of decision makers, no matter how highly placed they are. If an education system is to change its ways, it needs organizational learning rather than learning by a single individual placed at the top. There are two reasons for this. The first is that implementation of policy and even policy definition involves multiple participants. The second is that ministers of education and senior staff normally have a tenure too short relative to the time it takes educational innovations to influence learning conditions. The type of learning that we propose in this book is not one where one person—the expert— teaches and others listen, but is one of learning by discovery. Dialogue is an essential condition for that learning to take place. The expert must be willing to participate in this dialogue at a table with other stakeholders. The expert has a rightful place at that table, for the quality of the dialogue can be improved by this participation but only with the recognition that the conversation has been going on before the expert's arrival and will continue when the expert departs.

Chapter 2

What Do We Mean by
Informed Policy Making?

Policy is defined generally as a statement of the actions to be preferred in the pursuit of one or more objectives of an organization.
The term has its Latin origin in *polis*, referring to city or a people.
Some languages (e.g., Spanish) use the same word to refer to policy
as to politics (*política*). A recent trend is to define policy as what
organizations do. If we used that definition we would then require
a term to explain why organizations do what they do. In this book,
policy is defined as plans of action that contain both whys and whats.

Some writers treat policy not as specific solutions to concrete
problems but as frameworks for action. These may be in the form of
convincing interpretations of facts (Lynn, 1989) or convincing stories (Doron, 1986). Kelly and Maynard-Moody (1993) argue that
"policies themselves are now considered as largely symbolic, a way
to give voice to latent public concerns" (135). They link their position with Reich (1988), who argued that the prevailing ideal casts
government as a problem solver but that a more appropriate position is that policy making is "a process of posing questions, presenting problems, offering explanations, and suggesting choices"
(5). Education policy refers to the goals for the education system
and the actions that should be taken to achieve them.

Plan is often used to refer to combinations of policies specifying actions to be taken in time in pursuit of goals. Planning is dependent on policy analysis. Historically, however, planning has come to be associated with rigid recipes for action that ignore contextual and temporal variations and seldom work. *Policy analysis* has come into greater favor as it suggests a more responsive process, less subject to the difficulties experienced by comprehensive planning during the 1960s and 1970s. In fact, the terms have a common intellectual history and epistemology.

THE CONVENTIONAL VIEW OF POLICY, POLICY ANALYSIS, AND PLANNING

Conventional approaches to policy analysis and planning assume that it is possible to reduce uncertainty about the future by projection of the past. Knowledge of the effectiveness of previous actions can be used to predict the success of future actions.

In general practice, policy and plan are used to refer to statements of actions to achieve goals that affect all or most aspects of an organization. More specific statements are called programs or projects. It is common practice, therefore, to identify only top officials in the education system as policy makers.

In the conventional perspective, although the formulation of policies and plans can be done by isolated individuals or small groups, the intended results are always social or collective. Planners and policy analysts use their knowledge to identify the actions that others should take. In other words, those who make policies are seldom those responsible for their implementation.

This separation of knowledge and action is problematic conceptually as well as in practice. In most situations the persons who generate knowledge are not the same persons who formulate policy, who are not the same persons who carry out the policies. How is it possible for the policy maker to have the same knowledge as the researcher? How is it possible for the implementor to have the same knowledge as the policy maker? If we cannot know what determines others' behavior, we have no reason to expect that our understandings will be translated faithfully into the policies we would have specified, nor any reason to expect that our specifications of action will be carried out as we wish. In practice, policy makers have not followed policy advice from researchers, and policies and plans have not been implemented as intended. The highway of history is littered with abandoned plans. If policies and plans do not result in the actions and outcomes desired, what is their value?

Perspectives on Knowledge and Action

There are three general answers to whether we can know the determinants of others' behavior. Perhaps the oldest, dating at least to Plato, assumes that through the use of reason we can determine which course of action makes most sense in a given situation. All persons who reason will then adopt the same course of action. In Plato's view, those most capable of reasoning—the Philosophers—had the right to compel others to follow the most reasonable course of action. A second approach, which was formalized in the development of empirical science beginning with the Renaissance, specifies that the world is organized according to logical rules and that these can be discovered through analysis of how the world operates.

In their classic study on problem solving, Braybrooke and Lindblom (1963) suggest that the marriage of these two perspectives has resulted in today's rational-deductive approach in policy analysis. This is the dominant perspective on use of rational analysis and scientific information in policy formulation. We describe a third approach later which argues that we can only know the determinants of others' behavior by sharing those antecedents. In this perspective, knowledge is generated through action and shared knowledge comes best through shared action (and reflection on that action). For now, let us review the dominant or conventional perspective in more detail.

The most common answer to the knowledge–action dilemma proposes a solution based on the methods and assumptions of objective science. The explosion of knowledge during the Renaissance using the new methods of science encouraged rulers and their advisors to believe that just as it is possible to work out the laws that govern the movement of the heavenly bodies, so we can determine the laws that govern terrestrial organizations. Science, it was believed, would make it possible to escape the divisive and conflictual results of politics as a means for resolving social issues.

Critical to the development of this belief were giant achievements in mathematics. Leibnitz, Newton, and others showed that it was possible to represent with mathematic equations, using relatively few variables, the most complex of physical relationships. Why not, argued Destutt Tracy, develop a science of human economy in which all economic relationships will be expressed in mathematical form, giving us certain knowledge? He called his new science ideology. Meanwhile, Saint-Simon and Comte were developing the notion of a science of society, or sociology, that would reveal how best to organize society to achieve progress. In the nineteenth century a number of great thinkers built on these ideas. Darwin's explanation of the origin of human species not only further strengthened an argument for a materialist view of the world but provided a powerful metaphor for those seeking to justify the existing social order. Ernest Mach championed a unified science based totally on direct, or positive, sensory data that would provide a rational answer for all human questions. All nonobservable phenomenon were to be excluded from scientific discussion and dismissed as mere metaphysics, or even worse, philosophy.

Challenges to these perspectives came early in the twentieth century. New theories explained more than the old theories and used radically different assumptions about reality and our knowledge of it. But the achievements of Einstein with relativity theory and Bohr with quantum physics have only begun to affect how most people think about their world in recent years. Most of us, including most social scientists, still view the world from the perspective of Euclid (e.g., parallel lines never meet, the shortest distance between two points is a straight line, and 2 + 2 = 4) and Newton (reality is like a clockwork mechanism in which all gears are related by a fixed set of coefficients). Most social scientists, especially economists, are still trained to believe that it is possible to carry out value-neutral analysis, and that the best data are those that are universally true, that is, removed from history and context.

The Conventional Approach to Informing Policy Making

Policy analysis as a method for planning evolved from several different intellectual traditions associated with Newtonian physics and positivism. Linstone and Meltsner's (1984) genealogy distinguishes between a technical perspective (into which almost all policy analysts and rational planners are included), an organizational perspective (which emphasizes political processes), and a personalist perspective which grows out of psychological research. Policy analysis and rational planning are the children of systems engineering, systems analysis, and industrial organization theory. Friedmann (1987) names neoclassical economics, public administration, and systems engineering as the intellectual parents of policy analysis and rational planning. *Rational* has been preempted to apply to this kind of policy analysis and planning. This is an unfortunate choice of terms that has caused much confusion because all planning requires the use of reason and information to choose among alternative methods to achieve goals.

Each of those traditions shares a belief that it is possible to identify a limited set of empirical regularities that describe the behavior of systems, including human organizations, and that with knowledge of those regularities, organizations can be structured to run more efficiently and effectively. As these regularities are universal, they must be observable by everyone; that is, they must be objective rather than subjective. Objectivity requires the elimination of personal interest and politics.

Assumptions. Policy analysis emerged out of this tradition as a means of identifying those policies most likely to lead to goal attainment. The assumptions of policy analysis (generally implicit) included the following:

1. The Analyst/Planner (as individual or group) is located outside the implementing group and is therefore not affected by the forces that act on them.
2. The forces that act to condition or determine the behavior of the implementors are relatively stable and unchanging over time and therefore can be projected into the future.
3. The behavior of implementors is externally determined and therefore their own subjectivity or awareness is not relevant.

The identification of universal regularities or laws makes rational behavior possible. If we know how things work, the accumulation of information in the pursuit of goals makes sense. And if we know how things work, it is irrational for others to engage in behavior that analysis shows will not lead to desired outcomes. Therefore, the policy analyst can assume a nonpolitical or technical position, and he or she can stand outside the hurly-burly of human discourse. As a consequence, few policy analysts include political variables in their analyses.

Politics. Politics is an objective reality, a set of facts which has influence on how organizations operate. Shouldn't policy analysts include politics and political action in their analyses?

The distinction analysts make between political and technical bases for education policy analysis is not one of influence but of the validity of the information used to identify means to ends. In this case, *political* is often used as a pejorative, an ancient tradition dating at least from Plato who put politics and politicians on a lower level, further from the truth than the philosophers (today's scientists) who claim to rely more faithfully on reason and evidence in reaching their conclusions. Political data are never trustworthy.

Champions of this approach argue that, to the extent that we stick to the facts, we can avoid the introduction of any *-ism* which distorts our understanding and leads us away from effective planning. They say that reasonable people will agree on what the critical issues are, and careful research will indicate the correct responses

(Psacharopoulos, 1990). Planning is the derivative of analysis; its function is to identify those policies that will result in the most efficient allocation of resources. Planning and policy analysis use technical (i.e., supposedly nonpolitical) analysis and focus on means to achieve ends defined outside the planning process by politicians or policy actors (Psacharopoulos, 1986). Politics is sometimes included as an element in analysis but generally as an exogenous variable, or error term. Policy analysis often does not include political analysis.

The ostensible objective of planning from this approach is *plan making*, the presentation of a set of policies specifying objectives to be achieved and means to achieve them. The plan is said to fail when the results do not match the promises of the plan. Plans fail for two major reasons; namely, lack of political commitment and the substantive content of the plan.

Some analysts choose to ignore politics in their plan making. Rondinelli, Middleton, and Verspoor (1990) define political analysis as distinct from economic or financial analysis and cite research to the effect that World Bank project officers do more of the latter because there is so much to do.

As discussed, most plans and policies fail to live up to expectations for them. Recognition of the failure of policy analysis and planning was late in coming. One of the earliest American studies in implementation (Pressman and Wildavsky, 1979) found only one earlier systematic study of implementation (Derthick, 1972). Since that time, however, the field has bloomed and implementation is now a major concern with respect to policy analysis and planning. Implementation is treated as a separate process from planning, but planners and analysts are urged to take into account the lessons of implementation in their designs.

Implementation. Most work on implementation focuses on how to increase commitment to the plan by those responsible for its implementation. This research calls attention to a third reason for plan failure, often ignored by rational analysts: the process of making and carrying out the plan or formulating the policy. From this perspective, policies fail because insufficient attention is given to those who will be responsible for their implementation. For example, Warwick, Reimers, and McGinn (1992) describe failures in implementation of five innovative projects in primary education in Pakistan. Failure of analysts and planners to take into account aspects of the culture in which these innovations were inserted is a major reason for their rejection and failure.

The promise made by early implementation research was that with proper analysis and design, policies and plans could be written that would be successful. In other words, the success of planning depends on the planner or analyst. If he or she uses the right theory and the right methods and attends to issues of implementation, it will be possible to achieve the purposes he or she intends.

Repeated failures led to another view of reality. Policy was now seen not so much as a positive instrument that could be pursued faithfully to achieve objectives, but as a dialectical tool that would stimulate other processes, for which new policies would have to be developed. This can be seen in the following:

Implementation is evolution. Since it takes place in a world we never made, we are usually right in the middle of the process, with events having occurred before and (we hope) continuing afterward. At each point we must cope with new circumstances that allow us to actualize different potentials in what ever policy we are implementing. When we act to implement a policy, we change it. (Marjoe and Wildavsky, 1979, 191).

Different language has been employed by Warwick, who talks of the transaction that takes place in the process of implementation (Warwick, 1982).

Both of these perspectives signal a turning point in thinking about planning and policy analysis. Neither offers a methodology for an improved form of analysis, although Warwick offers a schema for detecting mistakes once made. However, they do suggest a view of policy formulation in which the policy maker or policy analyst is no longer removed from the situation but is intensely involved in it. Policy makers are actors as much as analysts, and influenced by others' actions.

POLICY AS THE RESULT OF ORGANIZATIONAL LEARNING

A major contribution to thinking about policy and implementation was the shift of emphasis away from policy intentions to action and actual change. Policies had been seen as disembodied from institutions and people. Now an appreciation has evolved for the centrality of organizations which design and implement policies. From an organizational perspective the distinction between a discrete planning or policy-making stage and an implementation stage is an artifact, a creation of the early literature of planning with little explanatory or prescriptive value.

Policy Making As Negotiation

Rationalist planning separates planning from implementation or knowledge from action. We propose an alternative in which policy is a continuous series of negotiations or transactions among stakeholders. In this perspective, policy is not formed in stages that skip from problem definition to analysis of options, selection of options, implementation, and evaluation. Rather, policy is formed as the product of competing internal and external interests. These exert pressure within and on the education organization to set agendas, derail ongoing efforts, mobilize resources, and influence outcomes.

Policy in this perspective is forged in the iterative interplay between declarations and actions. At some stages declarations are dominant, and at other stages actions dominate. Policies are formed rather than decided. Stakeholders for education reform do not alternate between discrete worlds of decision and action. Instead, they carry out their work and exert their influences in a seamless process in which planning and implementation blend. Change in education organizations is possible, not as an abrupt shift from one to another state, but as the outcome of ongoing negotiations where new ideas and practices find room amidst the old ideas and ways. This alternative view of policy leads to a different understanding of how education systems are controlled.

Conventional Thinking on the Impact of Policy

Conventional thinking argues that policies have a top-down influence on education systems. Implicit in this approach is a machine model of the educational system. Policies are conceived by some core of people and are implemented using an administrative machinery which can take orders from the top and translate them into changed conditions in the classroom.

This is not a caricature of an old and abandoned approach. Even current language evokes images of a machine model of the education system. Many education researchers, policy makers, donors, and advisors aspire to find the right policy levers to produce change in classroom. Education specialists have been searching for magic bullets that can bring about desired change in schools. While the specific magic bullets, the *content* of the prescribed change, may have varied over time, a pervasive trend of the conventional thinking about policy is the desire to find a blueprint of action which a well-tuned education machine can translate into new practices in schools and classrooms. This approach, centered in the content and specific actions to induce change, ignores the complex process by which change occurs. This operating style is an inadequate response to rapid changes in the external environment faced by most education systems, yet many systems operate in precisely this way as they think about managing educational change.

The paradigms we use to think about educational change act as self-fulfilling prophecies. Those seeking change behave in ways which reinforce their preconceptions about the nature of the education system. Any attempt to introduce change in the education system from the top (thinking of the organization in the framework of traditional administration) will evoke the responses which are appropriate to that traditional mode. It will create a traditional organization, good at carrying out orders and doing more of the same but woefully inadequate to generate real change. Initiatives which do not fit in the mold of what the education system has been doing in the past will be faced by resistance. The sources of resistance include the legal and normative framework within which ministries operate as well as the values and skills of teachers and administrators trained under the system which the new initiative or program is trying to change. We discuss this issue further in Chapter 3.

These sources of resistance freeze education systems; they block their capacity to respond to policy initiatives or to respond to change. The question then is how to unfreeze them. The rapid changes facing the world demand that schools be empowered as learning organizations to be able to initiate and manage adaptivity.

One way to open up systems to change is to think about them not as implementation machineries but as dynamic and complex organizations. We need to view educational change as a process which occurs in systems which are organic, consisting of multiple levels and networked by multiple relationships.

Changing the Unit of Analysis

Is there a role for planning, for policy analysis or for research-based information within this adaptive and dynamic view of organizations? Doesn't this complexity preclude any attempt to enlighten the choices made by institutions with the results of rational inquiry? Shouldn't we dismiss policy making as an exercise in futility and surrender to the notion that bureaucratic unpredictability and political chaos will carry the weight when it comes to shaping policy in action?

The answer to these questions depends on the unit and focus of analysis one takes. An individual policy maker trying to effect change in the education bureaucracy faces odds worse than those David faced when taking on Goliath. The challenge here is not to defeat the giant but is how to get the bureaucracy to dance to the tune of a different song. A magic bullet in the form of a policy prescription hitting the education bureaucracy in the middle of the head will be of no avail in this case.

A different way to put these questions in perspective is to shift the unit of analysis and look at them as if the organization is the actor. Can organizations be smart? Can they make choices that maximize utility? The evolving field of organization theory shows that it is indeed possible to overcome the common problem of groups which have a lower collective IQ than the sum of intelligence of their individual participants; that giants can indeed learn to dance (Senge, 1990; Kanter, 1990). Within this perspective there is a role for rational inquiry, for planning, and for policy analysis, but planning is understood as an ongoing conversation among the members of the organization (Flores, 1995). It is this conversation that defines the common vision which accounts for what organizations do.

Within this view, knowledge is a valuable resource to initiate and sustain change, but this knowledge is understood as the result of dialogue between multiple stakeholders who participate in the education system. Peter Senge (1990) has proposed dialogue as a tool to achieve meaning collectively, in order to further efficiency in business settings. We use dialogue here in the same sense, applying the concept to the education sector.

Knowledge in this perspective is a construction. It is the result of reflection on action, of sharing the result of that reflection, of creating common meanings about the processes which account for the action, and of alternative ways to organize collective action. Knowledge and action are inextricably linked in this perspective. Reflection upon action leads to knowledge which leads to action. The leap from personal knowledge to organizational knowledge requires dialogue.

The Importance of Social Process

This perspective views knowledge as a social construction in which social processes are fundamental to facilitate or impede knowledge and understanding. Trust is an essential condition to allow open dialogue. Trust makes it possible for participants to risk exposing their assumptions about the underlying processes which account for organizational action or which challenge existing operating procedures. Without trust it is very difficult to achieve a common vision in an organization. Other sociopsychological factors essential to nurture dialogue in organizations include faith in the potential of other participants in the organization and respect for self and others, which can encourage confidence, risk taking, and experimentation. Increased skills and competence also can increase the sense of self-efficacy which can allow open dialogue. Individuals have to learn so organizations can learn. The importance of sociopsychological factors to encourage this learning stems from the conditions which permit adult learning. Adults learn when they have no fear, when they have opportunities to reflect about their own practice, when they can dialogue with others to develop new ways to conceptualize their practice, when they can safely test and take risks to practice their new understandings and meanings, and when they can assess the results of their actions and go back to reflection and on to new action. These are also the conditions which facilitate learning among teachers, supervisors, and staff in ministries of education.

An important reason why policies do not reach schools is that there are no conditions to facilitate such dialogue and organizational learning. Education policies frequently fail to alter the reality of schools because senior education officials espouse a traditional paradigm of educational change which defends against critique. This paradigm blinds education systems to possibilities for change and officials end up doing more of the same thing. The paradigm is not without benefits: Many education systems have made remarkable efforts to expand their capacity. But the long-term consequences are a capacity that no longer matches possibilities.

The perspective we promote understands policy as a means to facilitate dialogue and reflection, so that the negotiations which shape the process of policy formation can incorporate the knowledge gained by all relevant stakeholders in the change process. The role of policy analysis and of rational inquiry is to enrich ongoing conversations that shape the policy. Different types of policy analysis and dialogue will be appropriate depending on the issues which they address.

Education systems face a variety of problems. Such variation calls for a rich topography of policy responses and approaches. The most effective agents of change are those who have maps to appreciate the diversity of this landscape; those who can call on a rich repertoire of approaches to find appropriate responses.

Dialogue Space

There is variation in the kind of education dialogue which helps organizational learning. We can think of dialogue as taking place in a space. This education policy dialogue space is defined by several vectors or dimensions. Different types of issues are placed in different points in this space and call for different types of dialogue. It is important to recognize where an issue fits in this space in order to carry out an appropriate dialogue.

Dialogue space can be characterized by finding the answers to five questions.

Is the problem to be addressed convergent or divergent? This is a distinction made by Schumacher (1977) about different types of problems for economic analysis. Whether a child can learn to read faster in her mother tongue or in a second language is a convergent problem. What to teach in the primary school curriculum is a divergent problem. Convergent problems have one single solution, divergent problems have multiple solutions. Sometimes the same subject may be investigated as a convergent or divergent problem.

Academic disciplines can simplify problems in order to find convergent answers, but it is important not to confuse the complexity of the real policy question with the simplification offered by technique. For example, a simple problem is whether the rates of return of primary education are higher or lower than the rates of return of secondary education. This is a convergent question that can be answered in fairly precise terms. However, that answer does not indicate what percentage of a country's education budget should be devoted to primary education and what percentage to secondary education, even if one chose to allocate the budget solely on the basis of economic returns. Those questions are divergent and complex. More than technique is required to answer them (Heyneman, 1995).

Is the information provided by the tools of a specific discipline sufficient to solve the problem? Some problems are fairly simple and can be solved within the domains of a specific discipline. Other problems are not simple and have multiple dimensions which call for multiple forms of analysis and for evidence from multiple disciplines. A large body of knowledge has been generated within specialized domains, such as experimental psychology and cognitive psychology. These define a fairly formalized theory of learning, or rather, theories of learning. But most education policy problems have dimensions other than the pedagogical dimensions, and therefore cannot just be solved resorting to learning theories. There are economic dimensions, political dimensions, organizational and bureaucratic dimensions, and legal dimensions. This is why policy analysis often has to draw from analysis of evidence derived from multiple disciplines and approaches.

Can the problem be solved by technical knowledge? All policy problems have a normative dimension. Certain situations are perceived as problematic by reference to certain goals, which in turn relate to values and to desired states. Sometimes problem solving occurs in a context in which it is not necessary to address the normative, and the exercise can concentrate on the technical aspects of analyzing evidence. For example, this is the case when there is consensus on the normative dimensions of a problem. It is the case when one is solving the problem from the perspective of a single decision maker, when one can assume the normative value framework of the decision maker and solve the problem within this framework. Some problems can be solved in this way.

For all problems, even those where solutions have to be negotiated among groups with conflicting values or normative frameworks, it is helpful for each party to identify a solution within their normative framework. This can clarify the options for negotiation and make dialogue possible. But this exercise should not be confused with solving the problem as if scientific knowledge had intrinsic normative authority. Technical knowledge alone is rarely sufficient to inform the direction of educational change. In many instances, the process of policy dialogue consists precisely of attempts to have reciprocal influence between political, normative frameworks and research-based evidence.

As discussed earlier, the literature on school autonomy is filled with ambiguity regarding the rationale for change. For example, is school autonomy or community participation instrumental to improve service delivery or is it a goal in itself? Is the main goal to improve service delivery or to redistribute power? How are possible tradeoffs between goals to be handled? Which goal should carry the greater weight? These obviously are not technical questions and require much dialogue among stakeholders.

Is there a single decision maker or are there multiple actors who will influence the policy decision? Certain policy areas can be influenced by fewer actors than can others. For instance, changing the foreign exchange rate of a country involves relatively few decision makers; changing the curriculum as implemented in primary schools involves many more actors.

In what context does the dialogue takes place? Some contexts are highly authoritarian and presume that decisions are made by highly-placed individuals at the top. Other contexts value democratic exchange and discussion of options prior to decisions. Some approaches to policy dialogue are a better fit to authoritarian contexts and other approaches are a better fit to democratic contexts. It is important to identify the context in which dialogue will be held.

From these five vectors characterizing the types of learning which foster organizational learning emerges a different understanding of the conditions necessary to obtain sustained and systemic education change. A fundamental requirement of change is creating consensus among key stakeholders on the need for change and the goals for change. For example, lasting educational change cannot be imposed on teachers who ultimately have a lot of autonomy in how to spend their time with their students. Teachers and parents have a fundamental stake in how education is provided and in what is taught. If they do not understand why change is necessary, implementation is problematic.

From this perspective, teacher-proof reforms are an absurdity. The two kinds of reforms are those which teachers and parents understand and support and those which they oppose. In a democratic context, the latter are not viable. It follows that policy formation should design processes which respect the rights of parents, teachers, and other key stakeholders to participate overtly. Change in practices will only happen if individuals learn new ways and if they can support each other in doing it. This requires that the new ways make sense to them and that this new knowledge is integrated with their prior sets of understandings and experience. Adults learn better in settings which respect them and which promote dialogue. Just as it would be absurd to attempt an adult literacy campaign assuming that an illiterate person has no prior knowledge, it makes no sense to assume that parents or teachers are ignorant. Their knowledge and sets of understandings are as important as those of the experts in drawing knowledge from research to shape policies which make sense.

If local actors are recognized as important stakeholders of education change, policy has to be adapted to local circumstances. What makes most sense in a particular context or education community may not make sense in another. This challenges the effectiveness of the magic bullets and blueprints.

Policy changes cannot be ruled by decree. Change takes time. Unfortunately, too many education reform proposals expect too much change from teachers without giving proper consideration to the new skills and understandings that must be developed for all key stakeholders to be able to participate in the intended change state. Failure to allow time for the development of these skills and understandings leads to frustration and to resistance to change.

Chapter 3

Why Education Policies Are
So Difficult to Inform

The realization that policy change cannot be disembodied from the actual organizations that will implement the change leads us to focus on the nature of education systems. We need to understand the characteristics of education organizations if we are to be successful arranging conditions that allow them to learn. The explanation of how education systems work depends as much on an understanding of vested interests, administrative routines, and bureaucratic inertia as it does on policy options.

We understand a national education system as an array of organizations loosely articulated to deliver various kinds of services to clients at different age levels in a wide geographic area. Legislation generally defines the aims and structure of national education systems, sometimes ambiguously. Government agencies typically employ a large group of people to work as teachers and administrators at different levels in order to deliver education to people of a wide range of ages in many different settings. Two defining features of education systems are their complexity and the complexity of the external environment where they operate. This chapter discusses these sources of complexity in order to understand the way education systems behave.

THE COMPLEX INTERNAL STRUCTURE
OF EDUCATION SYSTEMS

Education systems are among the most complex organizations in today's world. In most countries they involve directly more employees (teachers and administrators) or beneficiaries (parents and students) than any other public or private organization. They are differentiated by the destination of graduates and early leavers at different levels, by the characteristics of students and their families (special education, rural–urban, age of students, public–private), and by demands of other organizations who employ graduates of the system (i.e., technical, vocational, different university careers, and so on).

There are multiple levels in the structure of these systems; namely, national, state, municipal, and school. Actors at these many levels interact in various ways: Teachers interact with parents, as well as with national supervisors or local politicians, and senior administrators in ministries of education interact with national politicians, with teacher unions, with delegations of teachers or communities, and with associations of schools (i.e., private, religious, and so on). Effecting change in these complex systems and achieving the kind of shared vision we have discussed as necessary for organizational learning is a daunting task, to say the least. Yet this is necessary if policy reform is really going to signify changes in opportunities to learn in educational institutions.

Many education systems have a poor record of performance in terms of effectiveness, efficiency, and equity. While the specific constraints on effective design and implementation of education policy need to be analyzed in particular contexts, we need to examine some of the common weaknesses.

Common Weaknesses

Inadequate Funding of Education. In some cases this includes insufficient levels of spending. In other cases it includes regressive spending with emphasis on the higher levels of education which are attended disproportionately by the nonpoor. The combination of both cases compounds the problem of insufficient spending for the poor.

Insufficient Information and Analysis. Education policy is designed and implemented in many countries without the most basic information about the intended beneficiaries, the options that can best achieve certain objectives, or the actual impact of the programs implemented. The lack of this basic information on needs, effects, and costs prevents decision makers from using public resources optimally based on the actual needs of the population.

Inflexible and Inefficient Bureaucracies Characterized by Excessive Centralization. These bureaucracies lack assessment and follow-up mechanisms, are highly inefficient, and are generally overstaffed. Overall salaries are low and staff get in each other's way. Staff are generally concentrated in urban areas. Personnel systems have few incentives for innovation and improved performance. In large, centrally managed organizations, such as ministries of education, the means take priority over the ends. Often, there is also poor horizontal and vertical coordination and integration. Units within the organization end up seeking survival rather than achieving the objectives for which they were created.

Absence of Mechanisms to Make Officials Accountable to the Intended Beneficiaries of the Policies or to the Electorate. There are few mechanisms by which the intended beneficiaries of education programs can participate in the identification of their needs or in the consideration of options for policies or programs, and beneficiaries rarely have input in the evaluation of policies or decisions about whether to continue or terminate them. The question of accountability is complex because there is no simple answer to the question, To whom and for what must education officials stay answerable?

Education policy decisions are made and implemented without serious attention to their impact on effectiveness, efficiency, or equity. This stems from deficient ability to conduct technical analysis, as when ministries of education lack mechanisms to figure out where to locate new classrooms to satisfy enrollment demand. However, the lack of attention can also be attributed to a political economy in which those who make decisions do not suffer consequences from the groups who lose by those decisions. Also, there are constraints posed by goals and structures, personnel practices, and budget processes.

Goals and Structures

One of the peculiarities of education systems is that their goals are often hazy and multiple. The question as to whom should an education system be accountable does not have a precise answer. What is it that education systems are supposed to do? The multiple stakeholders whose interests are affected by an education system are likely to have more than a single view about the goals of a given education system. To some an education system will be a mechanism to increase national productivity, to others it will be a mechanism to foster national unity. Some will see an education system as a tool to promote social change, others will want education systems to ensure political stability, and others will see these views as too utilitarian and will instead want education systems to deliver education as a basic human right. The difficulties in reaching a single answer to the goals of education systems illustrate the divergent nature of most significant questions faced by education policy makers.

The reason why educators have difficulty answering what it is precisely that they would like to accomplish is not because they are stupid or incompetent. It is because they are trying to do many different things, because those things vary in different communities and for different teachers, and because many of these things relate to a fundamental aspect of the human experience: recreating culture, an issue which in itself raises many complex questions, namely, whose culture and for what purpose. Education systems would be easier to understand if there was a simple bottom line to check performance. One could then compare the relative merits of different strategies, structures, and practices by reference to how well the bottom line was doing. But that simplification will find little resonance in the experience of those who have worked in real education systems.

Who sets the goals for education systems? Most countries have legislation which give mandates to education organizations. This legislation sets broad goals, sometimes defines the structures of educational organizations, and frequently assigns public funds to finance certain functions of those organizations. A national education law often is based on a constitutional mandate. Generally, it contains legislation on training for work, law for universities, legislation for private education, a charter for a ministry of education and other educational institutions, and an education budget. These set the boundaries of who should be educated, how they should, and for what purpose.

Legislation and structures are not only the foundations of education systems but they define the space within which change can take place. It is hard to fund efforts to universalize access to secondary education if the law defines compulsory education only until grade six. It is difficult to increase funding to primary education, in a context of declining public resources, if the law assigns a fixed percentage of gross national product (GNP) or of public expenditures to universities. It is hard to expand access to private schools if legislation makes opening or operation of private schools difficult. It is difficult to allow parents to choose among public schools if the legislation that defines access to specific schools is based on one's place of residence.

Educational legislation is often extensive, cumbersome, and contradictory. As the product of political processes and of history, a country's package of educational laws and norms is not necessarily consistent with current realities and may not be internally coherent. In light of this source of complexity it is easier for education organizations to do more of the same than to try something new. Legal advisors are among the most important figures in ministries of education and they are often seen by their colleagues in the ministry as a source of resistance to change rather than as agents of change. They are seen as resistant to change because they are better at finding the legal impediments to attempt change than at finding windows of opportunity for innovation. But most fundamental change in education calls for legal reform, involving legislative processes and politics as key agents.

Another source of resistance to change is the structure of the Ministry of Education. Many structures are highly hierarchical, preventing horizontal communication and promoting centralization and slow response to changes in the environment. The structure of most ministries is hierarchical, often delegating very limited power to subordinate levels. Networks to exchange information horizontally are rarely encouraged and managers often pass the buck to higher levels in the organizational structure. As a result, high-level managers are typically overwhelmed with far more issues than they can handle effectively.

Because high-level managers cannot devote enough time to promoting coordination among different units, it is very common to find instances where the right hand does not know what the left hand is doing. For example, we have seen ministries where a curriculum reform has no impact in operations in the units responsible for textbook production or for teacher training for several years, or ministries where new legislation or regulations on school management have no impact in the units responsible for school supervision for several years. A good deal of apparent lack of support or synergy between units reflects structural problems of coordination and communication.

Structures define not just functional roles and specializations but formal relations of authority. Once a box or series of boxes is created in the organizational chart of a ministry of education it is very hard to remove it. This is the reason why the structures of many ministries seem more like quilts to which patches have been added over the years. It is common to see duplication of functions, confusion about functions, and poor coordination and communication between different units. When the new minister and staff begin to work in a ministry of education, they do not start with a blank slate in which to draw an organizational chart. They inherit an organizational structure with a history that has great weight in defining the dynamics of the education system and the roles of those who work in it.

One of the most difficult changes is in the functions of the *inspectorate*, the system of pedagogical guidance and supervision that is found in almost all education systems in the world. This has to do with personnel issues that are discussed later, but it is also the result of the inertia generated by traditional structures and positions. Another very difficult structural change to accomplish has been decentralization. Ministries of education around the world have attempted to decentralize delivery of education services, but frequently decentralization has not been implemented because real decision-making authority, capacity, or funds have not supported the espoused goal to decentralize.

The territories defined by structures become power bases with a constituency—those who are employed in the unit—which is more receptive to marginal changes than to changes that threaten the existence of the unit. As a result, duplication of functions is common and procedures are often unnecessarily cumbersome. It is very common for teacher appointments to take several months and even longer for the first paycheck to be issued to the new teacher. This long sequence of steps does not necessarily result in better control. On the contrary, in many ministries there is a problem of ghost teachers, or people whose name is on the teacher payroll even though they do not teach. In one country in which we worked, teachers remained on the payroll for as much as a year after they had died or left the service. These problems of malfeasance can occur because central officials do not have good control over their systems.

A special problem of the structure of education organizations relates to projects funded by international assistance agencies, or from the president's or prime minister's office. These externally generated projects often create project implementation units as a means to overcome the sluggishness of the education bureaucracy. The project implementation unit may solve the funder's problem, but in doing so it restricts organizational learning, duplicates functions, and adds to the crazy quilt that lasts long after funding for the project has ended or has been withdrawn. We have seen a number of departments and units in ministries of education around the world with no apparent purpose other than to employ the staff working in that unit.

In addition to legislation and norms, ministries often prepare or participate in the preparation of plans of different sorts, namely, five-year plans, annual plans, projects, strategic plans, and others. Planning is carried out in a variety of ways. In some cases there are planning offices. In other cases there are offices for international cooperation and foreign-aided projects. In other cases the planning function is assumed by the directorate of administration and budgeting, and in other cases it is assumed on an ad hoc basis by different operational units designated by the senior leadership.

A common problem ministries face when they undertake educational planning is the poor information base to examine the performance of the system. Good information systems are rare. Most ministries lack adequate data and indicators to monitor the achievement of education goals and objectives. They seldom have a way to examine how education objectives are affected by inputs and processes. None of the ministries in which we have worked have had information about the costs of various inputs. The few ministries with data on basic indicators lack appropriate structural and functional lines of communication with those who are responsible for planning. Ministries of education plan using far less information than necessary to make appropriate analysis of the performance of the system and the options to improve performance, and using far less information than is available in different units of the ministry.

Another common problem related to the establishment of goals and objectives in ministries of education is that planning often becomes a ritual, with very limited impact on day-to-day management. Plans are made for symbolic reasons and are forgotten as soon as the plan document is ready. We have observed in only a handful of ministries that planned strategies and outcomes are used to check routine performance and operations of the ministry. Most ministries lack a culture of evaluation and of management based on setting clear objectives and performing activities to reach specific targets over a specified period of time.

Another problem with goal definition results when there is too much planning, or rather, too many competing plans. A multiplicity of projects, each with their own planning cycle, fails to operate under a common policy framework, leaving ministries with an array of disjointed priorities and proposed activities which exceed the institutional capacity of the ministry. Excessive planning of this type hinders rather than contributes to routine management.

Personnel

As important as the goals and structures defining education organizations are the staff who work there. Who are the teachers and administrators of a given education system? How are they hired? What are the factors that influence their appointment, assignment, and promotion? The answers to these questions are central to understanding the level of skill and commitment of those whose salaries account for most of the public education funds.

For many talented people, education is not an attractive career. The complexity of educational structures, the lack or the inadequacy of teaching statutes, and the low salaries and limited promotion opportunities of educators drive away those with other options. As a result, there are many cases in which those who opt to teach are not the best and brightest or the most persistent of a given generation. In many cases, a significant part of the managers of the education system, especially but not exclusively at the lower levels, are teachers who have come up through the ranks. Teaching rarely provides a structure that allows professional growth for those who remain in teaching. In order to improve responsibilities and benefits, teachers have to go out of teaching, becoming principals, supervisors, and eventually administrators in the Ministry of Education.

It is common for teacher and staff appointments, all the way from the lower to the higher levels of responsibility, to be made on the basis of criteria other than the competency of the candidates or institutional requirements. As the largest employer in the public sector, the Ministry of Education is a desirable source of patronage to reward the political friends of those in power. This has three consequences. First, it reduces the available pool of candidates with a high probability of selection or promotion, leaving those candidates with a powerful political patron. These may not be the best qualified. Second, it reinforces a double standard as a code of conduct, in which staff know that merit and performance are not the preferred modes of organizational ascent. The third consequence is that it diminishes overall efficiency of work groups; incapable individuals reach positions of authority where they have to manage the work of others. As a result, recruitment, promotion, and incentive systems (monetary and nonmonetary) often prevent education bureaucracies from hiring and retaining capable staff. In many cases old legislation and norms make the political and practical cost of firing incompetent staff very high.

A common problem of ministries of education is the lack of competent managers. Most people who end up as school principals, supervisors, and middle- and high-level administrators were trained only as teachers. They were made managers because of seniority or because they had political connections. Of course, there are some managers who are competent and skilled to perform the functions for which they are responsible. There are no systematic studies of the managerial capabilities of ministries of education. We have worked in some well-run ministries; many are not well run.

One result of poorly qualified staff is that many education bureaucracies are incapable of meeting the technical and legal requirements of an ambitious program of change. Many ministries are incapable of sustaining an effective dialogue with ministries of finance to ensure an adequate flow of resources to fund change initiatives. Many lack the skills to engage other groups in society in dialogue and collaboration about a program of change. Incompetence leads to low self-efficacy, insecurity, and a willingness to retreat into more centralization in decision making, reinforcing the problems of centralized large bureaucracies.

Poor personnel practices compound the problems of rigid and dysfunctional administrative structures. The dynamics of ministries of education are often better understood through the lens of political, family, or clan loyalties than through the lens of administrative structures and procedures. The influence of these loyalties debilitates the culture of management, making it more difficult to organize collective action to seek the achievement of specific targets in a prespecified period of time. Unspoken targets and strategies such as fostering the power of a common political patron often prevail over the goals and objectives spelled out in legislation and education plans.

Ministries of education are not alone in their problems. They share these constraints with other agencies in the public and private sectors. Efforts to try to break the organizational culture defined by these practices face a lot of resistance not just from staff and history but from the external environment in which ministries operate.

Reformers often underestimate what it takes to help people learn to do things differently. There are many examples of how the training needs of teachers are often neglected in efforts to change the curriculum or instructional technology. Similarly, most reforms take for granted the administrative competencies of managers rather than create opportunities to develop them.

Another personnel constraint faced by ministries of education relates to the relatively low status of and high turnover in many senior administrative positions. Education is a profession where expertise does not seem to be immediately valued by the public. Most people who have attended school or who have children who have attended school feel competent enough to give opinions about what is appropriate or about best practices. This is true even for convergent problems which the lay person has no special expertise to solve. Lay people are less likely to claim expertise in professions such as engineering, law, or medicine. People who ordinarily cross bridges or use elevators do not think of themselves as having expertise to solve technical problems with bridges or elevators.

It is common to see ministries of education led by people of a diverse range of professional backgrounds and experiences each bringing their own personal preferences and theories about the best way to improve education. When this happens in highly centralized systems of decision making with limited opportunities for dialogue with other stakeholders and with limited checks and balances, problems grow more serious. Tragically, many of the ministers of education in the world have little familiarity with the public education for which they are responsible. They never attended public schools, nor did their close associates or their children. Those few ministers who had once been teachers seldom if ever taught in primary schools.

For various reasons, the average term of office of ministers of education is relatively short, less than a year in some countries. In countries where education is not a priority, ministers seek more promising appointments. Where education is a priority, ambitious politicians stay long enough to start a reform program that attracts public attention.

Although this turnover affects morale among high-level professional educators, it has relatively little effect on actual practice given the complexity of the bureaucracy. Lower-level functionaries have developed a myriad of ways to dissipate forces for change that come down from higher levels. The cost of leadership turnover is that it restricts the development of frameworks or institutional memory about the consequences of innovations from above. These shifts also make the more permanent staff in the bureaucracy skeptical about change. The frequent changes of ministers of education and other high-level staff creates organizations with extremely short memories. Turnover reduces the capacity of the ministry to negotiate successfully with organizations in the ministry's environment that have more stability of leadership. The teacher unions and other ministries such as finance or planning have the upper hand because their leadership is not new to the job.

Teacher unions are an especially important group in understanding the dynamics of education organizations. Commensurate with the large body of people they represent, unions share some of the challenges of large-scale ministries of education. Though conditions vary from country to country, many unions have, over time, lost touch with the concerns of their affiliates and have become, in practice, a regressive force in defense of the status quo, rather than a force of change. This is particularly the case for unions which have abandoned democratic means to select leadership and to develop their agenda. Given that union leaders are the survivors of long processes aimed at their intellectual, ideological, and sometimes physical annihilation, it should not be surprising that the quality of the arguments advanced by many unions, or their negotiating tactics, often seem to detract from educational opportunity, rather than to advance it. Many traditional and not very democratic unions are a hindrance to educational change.

Given their own weak capacity, most ministries of education can do no better than to preserve an equilibrium with teacher unions, with limited regard for their impact on educational opportunity at the school level.

Budgets and Funds

A budget is the backbone of any education plan, but most plans made by ministries of education have no secure financial backing. Education planners often do not know how much money will be available during the academic year ahead. Given large unmet needs, it is common for education managers to claim that education funds are insufficient. Why do some education systems spend less money on education than necessary? A simple answer is because they do not have enough resources. It is also because ministries of education do not know how to spend well and spend on time.

The budget process is loosely coupled with the process by which ministries of education formulate priorities. The best predictor of a country's education budget is not the priorities stated in the education plan but last year's budget. Usually, annual budgeting cycles are exercises of marginal changes to what was forecast for the previous year. In a few countries the next year's budget is based on actual expenditures one or two years earlier. In many countries these data are not available so the budget is made by assuming an incremental increase in last year's request. Instances where the education budget follows or is developed iteratively with a statement of educational goals, objectives, and strategies are extremely rare.

There is a logic to this. In many poor countries, salaries account for 85 to 95 percent of the total expenditures on education. As public-sector employees, teachers and administrators have either tenure or multiyear contracts. In any given year, between 85 and 95 percent of the education budget is encumbered; that is, it must be spent in a specified way. This is the most fundamental source of inertia in education. Ministries can only do more or less of what they have done in the past since this is all that the budget allows them to do.

This is the reason why foreign-aided projects are important. Even though they generally represent a very modest portion of total education spending, they provide the most freedom to fund programs away from tradition. In search of ways to finance innovations or quality improvements, many countries seek foreign assistance in the form of grants or loans. These expand the degrees of freedom of ministries when they result in increases to the education budget. At times, however, education loans are secured as budget support to fund activities within preestablished budget ceilings for the sector. In some cases, they provide funding for special perquisites such as travel to see education reform projects in other countries. Most often they provide training for staff to carry out new functions and training to teachers in new ways of instruction.

These grants and loans generally have the effect of expanding the activities of the ministry, increasing the total amount of revenue required. This may not be the intention of the donor or lending agency, but it is generally impossible for ministries to stop what they are doing in order to do something else. Almost all externally funded projects create parallel activities with parallel staff. The ministry has two options: (1) It can attempt to persuade the legislature to increase overall spending on education, or (2) it can kill old projects. The latter is politically difficult. Unless ministries make provisions to gradually incorporate in their regular budget the items financed with the foreign-funded project, the change processes will not be institutionalized. There have been many textbook projects which died as soon as the donor funding for paper ceased and many data and information systems projects stopped when local financing could not pick up computer maintenance or supplies.

The office of the budget in the ministry of education is usually more focused in dialogue with the ministry of finance than in dialogue with other technical divisions within the ministry of education. It is rare for education budgets to be prepared on the basis of a clear statement of objectives and programs of activities to achieve those objectives.

Educational plans rarely assess the cost effectiveness of various options for improvement and usually speak a language different than that which is spoken in the ministry of finance. Education plans typically justify goals in terms of social demand while ministries of finance are typically concerned with budgetary ceilings. The dialogue between education and finance is a series of negotiations to define the ceilings for the sector's budget. Because ministries of finance are, in many countries, concerned with administering scarcity, and because ministries of education cannot think and make proposals using a language which can effectively engage staff in finance, education generally receives less funds than it deems necessary to carry out its programs.

Excessive bureaucracy and regulations in finance and in education delay the release of assigned funds. For example, there is generally very limited flexibility to transfer funds from slow-spending accounts to fast-spending accounts. Given that many budgets are developed with excessive detail in programming expenditures for specific accounts, and given the loose coordination with the operating units discussed, it is common to see units paralyzed because they run out of funds while other units have more funds than they can spend. Ironically, these excessive regulations do not necessarily improve proper use of funds. A factor which sometimes delays the release of funds for their intended purpose is that those funds can be used as short-term investments in order to generate interests to finance various causes external to those for which they are intended. We know of several instances where contributions to political campaigns have been financed with the interests generated by investing education budgets in quick-return schemes.

The slow release of education funds by ministries of finance is a way to reduce the capacity of the bureaucracy to perform some of its activities. A ministry of education cannot spend the funds it should have spent in twelve months in the last six months of the year. Slow fund release also erodes the purchasing power of those funds. Delays in teacher payments, a common problem in many countries, force teachers to get in personal debt to attend to their basic life necessities. The higher than commercial interest rates set by local vendors and landlords take a heavy toll in the salary of the teachers. Anticipating delays in payments, many suppliers of services to ministries of education—constructors, providers of textbooks, and others—include markups in their prices as a way to offset the value of the capital that they will sink until they can be paid for their services. Timely payment of services and salaries is so rare in many ministries that it serves as an incentive for eager employees or providers of services to offer a cut to the officials responsible to disburse the funds in exchange for release of their payments.

The lack of synchrony in the preparation of the education budget and in the programming of education activities, when they are planned, along with the poor integration and coordination of activities of different units, makes effective delivery of education services difficult. For instance, it is common for school supervisors not to be able to supervise schools because the funds for transportation or per diem are not available. Sometimes schools are built but teachers cannot be appointed because school construction has not been coordinated with provisions for teacher appointments or for providing basic supplies to the school.

The root cause for many schools in ill repair, where teachers have no supplies to teach, where textbooks arrive but teachers have no chalk, or where new classrooms are built but new furniture never arrives, are the harsh financial realities faced by ministries of education. These include insufficient funding, funding poorly coordinated with the process of setting education priorities, slow delivery of funds, and funds sometimes used for purposes other than those intended. In many cases, local communities make financial contributions to the school. When these funds have to be entered into the treasury, the same delays ensue with the release of funds as they do with the rest of monies allocated to the school.

Looking at education systems as organizations helps us see that there is a long path from informing policy change to effecting policy change. Good ideas are only an input in a long process of organizational change. There are many features of education systems which become the bolts that lock the door to change. Bureaucratic inertia and routine do not paralyze the system; they keep it doing more of the same. This should not be underestimated because education systems, especially in developing countries, have achieved large gains in expanding access to education during the last three or four decades. But this ability to do more of the same is problematic given the changing external environment of education systems and given emerging needs for flexibility and adaptivity. The key is to unlock these large and complex systems, with their multiple goals and inadequate structures, poorly staffed and with poor budget processes, and to help them learn from experience and enable them to change.

Before we address how to open these locks, we need to turn to another source of complexity of education systems: the external environment where they operate.

THE COMPLEX EXTERNAL ENVIRONMENT OF EDUCATION SYSTEMS

Education policies are difficult to inform because so many different groups are interested in forming them. A proposal to update the curriculum in mathematics, for example, attracts the attention of textbook publishers, classroom teachers of mathematics, employers who require certain levels of mathematical ability in their employees, parents concerned about admission of their children in the university, university departments of mathematics, and others who are concerned about the outcome and feel they have a right to speak. Each group attempts to shape the policy to represent its interests.

These groups are called *stakeholders*. Their inclusion in the decision process is now widely accepted as an important method for increasing information for decision making and for increasing commitment to decisions once made. The concept has been most widely used in business management and evaluation research.

Development of the Stakeholder Concept

The concept of stakeholder was first published in 1965 (Ansoff, 1965). Stakeholder participation was featured in Ackoff's early work on strategy for corporate redesign (Ackoff, 1974). Today, stakeholder analysis is recommended in many texts on corporate management, especially for strategic management and planning (Alkhafaji, 1989; Bryson, 1990; Godet, 1991; Hatten and Hatten, 1988; Stoner and Freeman, 1992). Business management proponents of the use of concept argue that information about stakeholders, who make up the environment of the organization, can enhance achievement of organizational goals. Active involvement of stakeholders in organizational planning and decision making increases the likelihood of successful action. Recently, the concept has been used to critique the ethics of business practices (Collins, 1989; Langtry, 1994) and to propose a form of business organization controlled by stakeholders (Schlossberger, 1994; Weiss, 1994).

The concept of stakeholder analysis was first used in program evaluation in the 1970s by the National Institute of Education in efforts to improve program design and management (Bryk, 1983; Stake, 1975). Enthusiasm for involvement of stakeholders in evaluation design and implementation has grown steadily. A recent review of research on participatory evaluation lists more than eighty references (Cousins and Earl, 1992).

There are many arguments that are given in support of involving stakeholders in the evaluation process. One is that decision making can be improved by increasing information about the range of concerns, objectives, and commitments of intended beneficiaries of programs and about alternative means to meet those objectives and concerns while sustaining the commitment. For example, involvement of parents in design of a new curriculum unit may alert planners to sensitive topics that should be avoided. Teachers may be able to suggest alternative ways to organize the unit. Another argument is that involvement of groups interested in the process and the outcome of programs increases the understanding of those groups about the objectives and constraints, heightens the legitimacy of whatever policies are finally chosen, and contributes to mobilizing support for policy implementation. The benefits of involvement of stakeholders in the planning and decision process are recognized by those who operate within the critical realist perspective and those who are constructivists (Maxwell and Lincoln, 1990). There have been at least four applications of stakeholder analysis outside the United States (Bamberger, 1991; Lawrence, 1989; Salmen, 1989; Thompson, 1991).

Informing stakeholders requires knowing who they are and what they are interested in. Relatively little work has been done on the development of methods to identify stakeholders and their interests. In the business field, an early study by Rhenman (1968) suggested a stakeholder grid, a matrix that arranges stakeholders according to their source of power (i.e., formal or voting, economic, or political) and the kind of stake in an organization's decision (i.e., equity, economic, or influence). Various stakeholders are compared with each other in terms of direction of influence on economic, technological, political, social, and managerial dimensions. Another approach defines stakeholders as either supporters, uncommitted, or opposition, and then asks about the actions, beliefs, cooperative potential, and stakes of each group (Hatten and Hatten, 1988). The central part of Godet's (1991) strategic planning approach is the use of a series of matrices to determine the relative power and relative concern of various stakeholders about critical issues. But most studies in the business field make no reference to how stakeholders were identified.

In program evaluation, most methodological work has been done on techniques for obtaining information from stakeholders (Brandon, Lindberg, and Wang, 1993a, 1993b; Hallett and Rogers, 1994). One of the few lists of groups that should be included as stakeholders was the one done by Weiss (1983). In most publications, selection of possible participants is ad hoc and is based on specific circumstances rather than derived from a formal method of identification. With few exceptions (e.g., Timar and Kirp, 1989), there is no attention to what groups have been left out of the analysis and the consequences of this exclusion. For example, in one study participation in the development of an educational performance monitoring system was limited to superintendents, school board members, teachers, and representatives of professional education groups. No mention is made of who was left out (e.g., taxpayers who are not parents and evaluation professionals) and the possible impact of their absence (Henry, Dickey, and Areson, 1991).

Some attention has been given to the stages or moments in which stakeholders should participate in the evaluation process (Ayers, 1987). There has been no systematic attention to the most appropriate moments for involvement in policy formulation and planning processes, nor has there been attention to the most appropriate moments for participation by different categories of stakeholders.

The lack of attention to process is, according to Kelly and Maynard-Moody (1993), the result of overreliance on the positivist approach to social science. They offer a postpositivist critique that emphasizes the construction of meaning by participants in the policy process. They suggest that it is essential for effective stakeholder analysis to overcome the decontextualization inherent in the use of objective methods. They redefine objectivity as the result of a process of recontextualization that produces intersubjective agreement.

The most sophisticated set of procedures for stakeholder analysis is that developed by Reich and Cooper (1995). The procedures are called *Political Mapping* and are presented in text form as well as in a Windows-based interactive software program. The method proposes to identify "all aspects of public policy—what gets on the agenda, who supports an issue, who opposes an issue, whether an issue receives official approval, and whether the official policy is implemented" (Reich and Cooper, 1995, 5). The procedures originally were developed to identify stakeholders for various kinds of health issues, namely, a health care reform. All data are supplied by the user of the Political Mapping tool. The procedure begins with identification of the main decision or policy statement. The user then specifies the goals, mechanisms, and indicators of the policy. The procedure requires the user to identify the type of stakeholder (e.g., organization, social group, or individual), their position with respect to the policy, the strength of their position, their power (made as a subjective judgment by the user), and the extent to which power is concentrated on this issue or diffuse. The user then lists various consequences of implementation of the policy and indicates which of the stakeholders would be affected and to what degree. Comparison of this information with information on which stakeholders are most important to the user suggests further questions with respect to the political feasibility of the policy and opportunities to influence that feasibility by coalition formation.

Political Mapping is by far the most advanced method for stakeholder analysis. However, it suffers from a lack of a conceptual framework. The model of political process underlying Political Mapping remains implicit, although it appears to be derived from a pluralist model and to assume that the political process is the same in all sectors. Pluralist politics are thought to dominate in the United States; but in countries with a more centralized tradition of government, the state plays a large role. Therefore, Political Mapping may have to be transformed to fit the reality of countries in which the state plays a dominant role in the political and policy processes.

Procedures for the Identification of Stakeholders in Education

Welsh and McGinn (1996) have developed a conceptual framework for the analysis of stakeholders in public education. The framework leads to a set of procedures for comprehensive identification of stakeholders, their relative importance to the policy formulation, planning and implementation processes, and the moments most appropriate for involvement by the different groups. The framework provides an excellent description of the complex external environment of a ministry of education.

Definition of Stakeholders. Stakeholders are defined as persons or groups with a common interest in a particular action, its consequences, and who is affected by it. All actors in an institutional context are potential or passive stakeholders. In education this includes groups as diverse as parents, children, Parent–Teacher Associations (PTAs), education faculties, taxpayers, teachers' unions, public service employees, public contractors, employers, professional organizations, and others. All these groups have an interest in setting the educational agenda and shaping the organizations which are established to participate in the process of educational provision.

In this process some actors are transformed from potential stakeholders to kinetic or active stakeholders. The kinetic stakeholders generally pursue their interests of the situation (context) of a particular organization within the institution. In this context stakeholders focus upon particular issues which touch directly upon their interests. It is here that toes are stepped upon and dancing partners found, as stakeholders enter into coalitions. The process can have transformational effects as coalitions see interests and possible effects not recognized earlier. The transformations lead to shifts in the organizational context. Welsh and McGinn (1996) note that little attention has been paid to the fact that stakeholders, chameleon-like, change with the context and change the context because they are learning by the activity of participation.

Categories of Interests. The interests or effects of action by stakeholders take three different forms and identify three categories of stakeholders. One set of interests focuses on the process of generating the decision, organizing a program, and managing a system. The concern is to produce something or stop it from being produced. The term generation can be used instead of production to avoid the implication that there is always a tangible product and that there is a final product closed to further learning and change. On the other hand, it is important to keep in mind that a major group of stakeholders focus their attention on the process of bringing into existence what is called education.

Examples of generation in education are the development of curriculum, printing of textbooks, and construction of buildings. Teachers produce or generate education when they develop curriculum but teaching someone else's curriculum is not included in this category. The first category of stakeholders are generators or producers.

A second set of interests and actions is concerned with the distribution of the product that is generated. This distribution sometimes involves an exchange of money, in which case the interest is in selling the product. In most cases, however, distribution is the delivery of education. Teachers may sometimes produce curriculum but more often are distributors; they deliver education. Education managers do not produce textbooks but are concerned about their distribution. Teachers may be involved in the process of distributing students among different levels but are not involved in the resource decisions which make a particular pattern of distribution possible. For some, privatization of public education means private control over the distribution of a publicly-produced curriculum. The second broad category of stakeholders is distributors.

A third set of interests in education focuses on the benefits to be derived from application of the product. Students and their parents use education to enhance the student's life chances as well as to improve the quality of his or her life. Employers also are users, as are a variety of other groups in society who expect the product of education to contribute to achievement of one of their objectives. It is important to note that it is the users and not the producers who finance education systems. Those who finance education systems are concerned more about the utility of the product than they are about how it is produced.

Any given person or group may occupy more than one of these stakeholder categories. For example, a person may be both a parent of a student (a user) and a worker in the ministry of education (a generator and a distributor). The owner of a construction firm is a producer and may also be a user concerned with the quality of graduates that he or she can hire. The expression of these interests will occur in different moments of time according to the process or cycle of policy formulation and implementation. As a consequence, the ministry of education experiences an unstable environment. The set of stakeholders attempting to influence ministry policy and action changes over time according to the issue and the stage of the process of policy making and implementation.

Moments in the Expression of Interests

Welsh and McGinn (1996) define six moments in the process of policy formulation and implementation. These are referred to as moments to indicate that they are transitory, though they may take place over days or weeks. Less important than the number of categories is the recognition that policy formulation and implementation is a complex, nonlinear, often recursive process that permits and attracts the participation of different persons and groups at different moments. The moments are illustrated by reference to development and implementation of a policy regarding secondary education in Jamaica. The six moments are: manifesto, policy, program, project, application, and assessment.

Manifesto. Manifesto refers to the result of discussions during that period of time when institutional and organizational stakeholders identify a concern or set of concerns that require action. Depending on the weight of these concerns, other institutional stakeholders may become involved. The magnitude of this concern progressively incorporates more institutional stakeholders shifting them from a potential position to a kinetic one, thereby bringing their institutional interests to bear. For example, debate over secondary education in Jamaica went on for several years, especially among the intellectuals and the bureaucrats of the institution, before the government finally decided to carry out a reform.

The kinetic stakeholders who participate in this moment are those that define themselves as having a right to define objectives for the education system. This is the largest group of stakeholders that gets involved in the policy formulation and implementation process. In Jamaica all sectors of the society participated in some fashion in the discussion about problems in the education sector. A variety of concerns were expressed. However, the government's action was in reaction only to the manifesto by stakeholders who demanded increased access to secondary education.

Policy. A smaller group is self-selected from the larger pool of kinetic stakeholders who develop their manifesto and is involved in the definition of specific goals to be pursued and the broad methods to be used in that pursuit. Not all potential stakeholders are familiar with the policy process or assign themselves competence in the definition of policies. Typically excluded from this process are groups that lack information about how education policy is formulated. Within the ministry, lower-level functionaries and teachers are excluded from policy formulation even though they are stakeholders. On the other hand, officials of teacher unions may be included in the process. The response to the manifesto in Jamaica was a policy decision to increase access to upper secondary education while leaving the established, elitist, high school system intact.

Initial policy choices touch off another round of public debate which may result in a reformulation of the manifestos articulated by political parties or submitted to government by stakeholders. However, the debate can draw more of the potential institutional stakeholders into the process. This debate process can enlarge the pool of organizational stakeholders who get involved in formulating the policy choice.

Program. The process of translating policies into programs is carried out by staff within the education organization, occasionally with the participation of experts and special interest groups from the larger institution. The latter often represent different levels of contexts, specifically the international, national, regional, and local levels. The allocation of the duty of program formulation activates potential stakeholders within the organization. In Jamaica, the participants in designing the Reform of Secondary Education (ROSE) program involved World Bank officials, staff from the national planning office, university professors, representatives from some but not all upper secondary schools, and policy level officials from the ministry of education. World Bank participation was preceded by an agreement (policy) that the World Bank would provide assistance to the secondary level while the United States Agency for International Development (USAID) and the InterAmerican Development Bank would provide assistance to the primary level. The group of stakeholders that designed the ROSE program chose a strategy of improving the quality of lower secondary schools so that more students would pass the examination that determines entrance into upper secondary schools. The process of program design is iterative and may include reformulating the general policy statement that touched off the process.

Project. The specific sets of activities that take place during programs are called *projects.* ROSE provides funds for improvement of existing lower secondary schools. Each school chosen for improvement is considered a project. The stakeholders that get involved at this stage generally are those groups immediately affected by each project. Because there is much more demand for entrance to upper secondary schools than can be satisfied in Jamaica, senior secondary officials do not attempt to influence the choice of junior secondary schools to receive additional inputs. On the other hand, local officials who did not participate in the design of the ROSE program are active in attempting to recruit school improvement funds for institutions in their district.

Application. As in all organizations, the persons who make policy decisions (including choice of schools to receive project funds) do not have the same interests as those responsible for the use of those funds. Project descriptions and plans often leave considerable leeway for intervention by implementors and local managers. The actions of these stakeholders are often not directly visible to many of the stakeholders who participated in decisions about the program or the policy. In ROSE, as in most other projects, what is done at the moment of application is not what was expected. The stakeholders who participate in this moment tend to do so as individuals rather than acting as representatives of formal groups. Application is the moment when stakeholders deformalize the policy and program while tailoring the project to their organizational context. Even at this stage in the progress, potential stakeholders are transformed into active or kinetic stakeholders. Sometimes, as in the case of teachers in Jamaica, they may have a common set of interests and values with the kinetic stakeholders who entered earlier, but this need not be the case.

Assessment. Assessments are inputs to discussions about the adequacy of policies, programs, and projects and may lead to their reformulation. For that reason, program officials often attempt to control assessments in their design and execution and in the dissemination of their findings. Assessments can also provide inputs for the debate that leads up to a manifesto. Not all programs include procedures and instruments to assess the implementation of the project in terms of the specifications of the program and the goals of the policy. Assessments can be focused on inputs, process, and outputs. Each kind of assessment affects a different set of stakeholders. In ROSE, for example, program officials are most concerned with whether inputs are being provided as planned, while those who participated in policy formulation are most concerned with whether admissions to upper secondary schools have increased.

Users are most likely to be dominant in the manifesto moment and to be consulted in the assessment and policy moments. Producers have most say in the policy, program, and assessment moments. Distributors in the education system have most influence in the project and application moments. The focus and intensity of interest of each group changes according to moment of the policy formulation and implementation cycle. However, the overall interest is defined by the tasks of the system that are affected by the policy in question.

External Involvement According to Category of Task

Education systems are designed to carry out four major categories of tasks. Welsh and McGinn (1996) identify these categories as: access, retention, classification, and placement. Education systems carry out the following tasks:

1. Recruit, select, and admit students
2. Attempt to keep them in the system long enough to have some transforming effect
3. Sort them into different tracks and levels
4. Certify them for and place them in institutions of the larger society

These are four policy domains. Different stakeholders get involved according to the particular policy domain in question.

Educational organizations and their suppliers are the producers of education and benefit directly from the increase of access. In addition to those directly employed in education and to the owners of educational organizations, this group of stakeholders includes: construction companies; companies that provide instructional materials including textbooks; vendors of uniforms, food, and other consumables; insurance companies; universities and consulting firms that provide technical assistance services; companies that produce and apply tests; and domestic and international agencies that thrive on the health or illness of the educational establishment. Each of these groups can be mobilized to support expansion of educational access.

Those involved in distribution are more interested in policies that affect the activities associated with policies of retention and classification within the system. For example, teachers are primarily concerned with issues that affect the way they distribute education; that is, work with students. These concerns are often defined in terms of quality but primarily affect the work that teachers are expected to do. Most teacher unions are organized primarily to provide what are considered suitable working conditions and compensation for teachers and to protect their jobs. The managers of education systems also may be concerned with quality but many focus their attention on the way the work of education is carried out; that is, on the process of distribution.

Some groups that appear to be interested in distribution issues (e.g., those who call for increased efficiency in education) are really concerned primarily with the production process. Although a nod is given to improving quality, the policies they back almost always involve doing the same with less, rather than doing more with the same. On the other hand, teachers can be mobilized to do more with the same, as has been demonstrated in the ability of some school-based management policies to increase teacher work and student learning with no increase in teacher pay. What is happening is that teachers are allowed to have a major say in the production of education and not just in its distribution.

Groups concerned with equality of educational opportunity, including parents and ethnic groups, have learned that they should focus as much on issues of retention and classification as on issues of access. The ROSE program, for example, is intended to increase classification of students into higher levels of secondary school by changing classification criteria.

Users are most interested in placement, but are also affected by policies that affect the volume and quality of leavers and graduates from the system. Their primary interest is in maximizing the quantity of high-quality leavers and graduates from the system. Given fixed resources, the expansion of access can reduce quality. Policies to retain students who do not do well raise unit costs. If job openings are few and there are many potential applicants, employers may well want the education system to impose classification policies that restrict the number of graduates.

SUMMARY

Education systems operate in complex and changeable environments. One day the ministry has to deal with one set of interest groups, and the next day a different set presents themselves. Of course, there are long periods of quiescence when little is happening. Once a group has become active and has demanded action by the ministry and once the manifesto has been proclaimed, the ministry faces rough seas. Traditional education bureaucracies, those with a high degree of professionalization (all staff trained in education), are not likely to have the conceptual frameworks or methodological tools to be able to keep informed of the motives and concerns of external groups. As a consequence, the ministry is often surprised by the actions of external groups which can block their attempts to get policies approved or implemented. Most difficult to anticipate are the actions of groups with headquarters and constituents outside the country; that is, the international agencies, foreign governments, and foundations that attempt to intervene in national education issues. With limited information, and even more limited capacity for political analysis, the ministry loses its titular position as leader of education policy. The ship of education is then adrift as various stakeholder groups fight for control of the helm.

PART II

Approaches to Informing Policy for Education

When schools were places where independent teachers offered their services, there was little use for formal research on education. The relationship between teaching practices and learning outcomes was visible enough to teachers and to their clients to make possible improvement in teaching and the outcomes attached to it. Of course, there was great variety across schools and in the individual teachers who taught in them.

Only when the Roman Catholic Church and nation–states became interested in standardization of schooling did research become important. The Church sought uniformity in belief, while the state sought loyal citizens at the lowest possible cost. Controlled experiments in different forms of schooling provided the answers and the first education system policies and plans. By the middle of the eighteenth century, the Church had learned how to provide basic education to large numbers of children. Novices with no prior skills in teaching could be trained to implement scripted lessons and to use standardized textbooks. The invention of the graded school by the French, and the design of education in Prussia based on observation of how children develop, were the foundation of today's mass education systems.

Research in education was modeled on the physical sciences, which in two centuries had generated enormous amounts of knowledge and transformed the conditions of human living.

THREE BASIC PERSPECTIVES ON
KNOWLEDGE UTILIZATION

Today there are three basic perspectives on the problem of utilization of knowledge in decision making. The first approach is older than Socrates but brilliantly captured in more recent times by Isaac Newton's metaphor of the clockwork universe. This approach defines truth as universal and unchanging. The information that a decision maker requires to be correct is everywhere the same, depends only on technical aspects of the particular issue, and can be obtained accurately by any person. This perspective champions a single, universal science, including a universal social science and a universal history that makes it possible to specify which courses of action will be correct.

The second approach may seem only a petty modification of the first but the modification has enormous political significance. This second approach accepts the universality of truth but points out that the correctness of a decision depends not just on technical aspects of the issue but on the objectives of the decision maker. It may always be true that A leads to B, but if someone is seeking C, A may not be the right answer. We can assess in advance the correctness of a decision, but to do so requires technical information and political information (that is, knowledge of values and objectives).

The first approach was dominant in education planning and policy analysis up until the 1970s. The failure of centralized and command planning systems challenged the applicability of Newtonian science to human affairs. Recently, the increasing popularity among physical scientists of relativity and quantum theory approaches to science have filtered into social science, providing new arguments against claims for universally applicable truths.

One manifestation of this shift in thinking is enthusiasm for decentralization of decision making. Initial proposals merely moved central decision makers applying universal recipes closer to schools and teachers. In recent years, there is increased diversity within national education systems, as provinces, districts, and sometimes schools are given autonomy to decide on curriculum, pedagogy, schedules, and qualifications of teachers.

This move is accompanied by calls for localization of knowledge; that is, for research to insure that local decisions will be correct using the knowledge appropriate for that circumstance. The specification in advance of which decisions are correct is still considered possible through rigorous policy analysis; that is, the scientific method. Truth is still universal and unchanging but it is no longer seen as singular. Once a decision maker has decided on the goals to achieve, technical aspects of the issue determine which policy should be pursued.

The third approach to knowledge and decision making begins with a new metaphor for human action. Instead of living in a clockwork universe built (by God) for all time, we participate with God in a process of creation, of construction of new realities. Truth is not a static quantity waiting to be discovered but something that we bring into existence through our actions. Today, we can know so much more than generations before us not because we are smarter but because there is so much more to be known. Through the actions of previous generations there are new truths to be discovered and known, and we will produce new realities and truths for generations to come.

There are some circumstances in which it makes sense to look for the correct way to get to a fixed goal. Routine activities have fixed goals, and therefore we can specify the best and most efficient way to achieve that goal. But in these circumstances we almost always know how to proceed; knowledge for decision making is not an issue.

In many circumstances, decision makers cannot specify goals with any clarity because what is being sought does not yet exist and is not known. We can distinguish here between innovation of new methods, in which the goal is known but we are looking for a better way to achieve it, and new projects, in which we seek something not yet experienced. If decision makers are unclear on goals, we cannot be certain as to which methods will be more effective or efficient.

In this third approach to decision making, knowledge changes as the object of the knowledge is changed by our actions. Truth is temporal and cannot be universal. Because truth is about human experience, it is necessarily particular. The problem of science is not how to discover universal truths, but how to enable individual persons to understand each other's particular truths. Science provides the means for collective action to build society not by indicating the one and only path that all must follow, but by providing a means for people to share knowledge and understanding and to build a common pathway.

The chapters in this section lay out the major perspectives on utilization of research knowledge in education. Chapter 4 reviews the tradition which emphasized the correct utilization of knowledge to define and resolve policy issues in education. This tradition was born in the somewhat unsuccessful experiences of social scientists and economists who sought to plan education to enhance larger societal objectives. We call this approach policy dialogue as communication and persuasion. A later tradition is reviewed in Chapter 5, which focuses on efforts to produce knowledge that would closely match interests and capabilities of decision makers. We call this approach policy dialogue as negotiation. Chapter 6 introduces the limited work that has been done working with decision makers on using methods of science to construct particular knowledge and then develop common understandings. We call this approach policy dialogue as participation and organizational learning.

Chapter 4

Utilization as Using
Precooked Conclusions

In this approach, research produces knowledge that can inform policy choices. The central question in this approach is, What can the researcher, as knowledge producer, do to influence the process of policy making? The perspectives within this approach range from those proposing efforts to increase the effectiveness of dissemination to those that propose advocacy and social marketing as ways to persuade policy makers. Common to these perspectives is the assumption that knowledge production and utilization proceed in stages. The first stage, in which knowledge is created, is the domain of the researcher. In the second stage—dissemination or persuasion—the researcher tries through various means to capture the attention of a seemingly passive decision maker in order to translate the results of research into policy more or less automatically. This chapter discusses some of the variations of this approach and presents decision theory which portrays the way decision makers operate in ways consistent with this view of dialogue as communication.

UTILIZATION AS DEPENDENT
ON INFORMATION DISSEMINATION

The early realization that research results did not automatically result in policy changes led to explaining the differences in cultures between researchers and decision makers (Dunn, 1980; Webber, 1991). Because content and meaning were considered properties of the message, the concern was how to present a message so that it would be received correctly. Torsten Husen, one of the key figures of the International Association for the Evaluation of Educational Achievement (IEA), which sponsored cross-country studies of educational achievement (the IEA studies), explains why education research fails to influence policy decisions:

A major reason for the disjunctions between researchers and policy makers is ineffective dissemination. Research findings do not by themselves reach decision makers and practitioners. Researchers seek recognition in the first place among their peers. They place high premium on reports that can enhance their academic reputation and tend to look with skepticism upon popularization. (Husen, 1994)

Mismatches between research and policy were explained as failures of communication. These were explained in terms of factors such as messages being too long, use of unfamiliar terminology, presentation of data in tabular form or using sophisticated analyses, and different timing for researchers and policy makers. After trying out various formats, researchers learned to use more graphs, to avoid technical terms, and to keep the message simple. These lessons were learned by observing which messages were best received and by asking the receivers to suggest how best to present information. The main challenge in this perspective is how to package the message obtained from research in the best possible way to capture the attention of the policy maker.

A review of the experience with several waves of IEA studies concludes that the impact was greater where researchers had established links with policy makers.

After the IEA Six Subject Survey had been completed and two years had passed, I was constantly asked about the "effect" of the studies. Had they really improved educational practice in the participating countries? I talked with the heads of the IEA National Centers. Of the twenty-one countries, something in terms of impact on legislation, curricular guidelines or policy action had happened in fifteen of them and nothing had happened in the other six. My general assessment of the reasons for this dichotomy was that in the countries where nothing had happened the researchers had no links with policy makers (or were too junior to attempt to forge such links). Again, my impression was that the researchers were either poor communicators with policy makers or were very good academic researchers and disdained the notion of communicating with mere *administrative* policy makers. Sometimes, the enormous task of communicating with policy makers, where each of the hundreds of school districts is autonomous, was a major deterrent. . . .

In some instances, it might have been the case that the policy makers just did not want to know the results or had not any established channel for receiving data which they, themselves, had not requested. (Postlethwaite, 1994, 197)

The rest of this chapter discusses one approach of how decision makers choose among options and two approaches used to package the research message, one spreading the message throughout networks that link researchers and decision makers and another orchestrating efforts of advocacy and persuasion.

DECISION THEORY

The decision theory approach to research utilization focuses on the process by which decision makers seek out and use information. It differs from the knowledge utilization models that focus on qualities of the information and how to improve them. Attention instead is on the rationality of the decision maker.

The elements of that rationality are succinctly captured in the following classic characterization:

When we first encounter him in the decision-making situation, he [the decision maker] already has laid out . . . the whole set of alternatives from which he will choose his action. . . . To each alternative is attached a set of consequences . . . the decision maker has a utility function or preference ordering that ranks all sets of consequences from the most preferred to the least preferred. The decision maker selects the alternative leading to the preferred set of alternatives. (March and Simon, 1958, 137–138)

Choices are rational to the extent to which they are guided by the information presented. The decision maker's task is to assign values to possible outcomes. Once that is done, the decision is determined by the actions of the researcher, who provides the information on the relationship between actions and outcomes. Failure of the decision maker to act on the information is a lack of rationality; it is irrational.

The validity, or truth value, of the research depends on the methods used. If they are objective, the findings of the research are true. Politics, political thinking, or any other insertion of subjectivity into the process subtracts from the validity of the research. Researchers have been bolstered by evidence that decision makers appear to support their belief in the importance of objectivity (Caplan et al., 1975). A survey reported that when decision makers rejected information provided by social scientists, they often did so because the study sample was inadequate or questionable analysis methods were employed.

When policy analysis came on the field around 1968 (Friedmann, 1987), it was introduced as a new science of design (Simon, 1969). Statistical decision theory, linear modeling, and artificial intelligence would provide the ram to break through to a new era of understanding and progress. A principal barrier to that progress was lack of attention to the effectiveness and efficiency of policies and plans. More important than what was being sought were the means used to seek it. Policy analysis was a universally applicable means to discover the truth.

The reliance of analysts on high-powered but sophisticated methods reduced the participation of clients who were unable to understand the methods being used and who did not welcome the methods in the pursuit of objectivity.

Applied economics, generally in the guise of benefit cost analysis, were assigned talismanic qualities in one of the leading policy texts, e.g., "Benefit–cost analysis is a methodology with which we pursue efficiency and which has the effect of limiting the vagaries of the political process." (Stokey and Zeckhauser, 1978, quoted in DeLeon, 1992, 126)

A limitation to the immediate application of this new insight to the improvement of education was the lack of rigorous studies on the contribution of specific policies to different goals. We lacked systematic information on what works. Prior to the 1970s, education planners had focused on identification of the goals that education systems should be expected to achieve. Emphasis had been on the importance of education as an unopened black box. Research dealt with barriers to the expansion of education to satisfy demand. Attention shifted to what kind of education should be provided, or to issues of quality instead of quantity.

Comparative research was seen as one means to identify quickly how to design an effective and efficient education system. The comparative method fit well with the logic of policy analysis and Newtonian science. The method assumes that there is one best way of organizing resources to produce such things as student learning. Variations in levels of student learning across schools are taken as evidence that there must be diversity, and therefore inefficiency, in patterns of organization of resources. Comparison makes it possible to detect which school is best organized, and this pattern becomes the solution to the deficiencies of all the other schools.

The first two national studies of this kind, by Coleman in the United States and by Plowden in Great Britain, were not immediately helpful, as their first readings suggested that little could be done to improve attainment of the goals set for those systems. Schools did differ from each other in levels of student learning, but not because of differences in their resource inputs. The long-term contribution of this early research was the generation of a large and increasing volume of comparisons of education systems (Heyneman, 1995).

The comparative method assumes universality of at least some of the properties of these systems. Only if they share similar structures and similar processes does comparison make any sense. The new research was motivated by a concern to find those policies that work across education systems. The BRIDGES project, for example, was originally described in a USAID project paper as being motivated by a hope to find the same kind of silver bullet that public health researchers has found for the treatment of dehydration in infants. The educational equivalent of a package of salts might be textbooks, new forms of teacher training, and perhaps even computer software.

The most extensive work of this kind has been done under the general sponsorship of the IEA. These studies compare across countries by using standardized achievement tests and standard questionnaires describing material inputs and practices in schools (both kinds of instruments appropriately translated). It only makes sense to compare the effectiveness of schools in Jordan and Sweden if we assume that the schools in both countries are only variants of a universal type of school.

Perhaps because education lagged behind other sectors in generating the kind of comparative data most useful for policy analysis, enthusiasm for the rationalist approach has continued in education even to the present. Criticisms of the component elements of policy analysis began to surface in other sectors beginning in the 1970s. One of the first victims was Programmed Planning and Budgeting Systems (PPBS). PPBS asked managers to specify measurable objectives for each of the programs for which they are responsible. Comparison of the inputs that are required to generate various levels of outputs indicates immediately which programs require assistance and which should be reformed or abandoned. Applications of PPBS, especially in the public sector, failed primarily because the goals of most organizations are much more complex than can be measured. They evolve over time, as do means to those goals (Wildavsky, 1975). The information policy makers use cannot therefore be anticipated in advance. PPBS and other variants on systems analysis worked only by forcing organizations into a universal and unchanging framework, perhaps initially relevant but increasingly distant from a dynamic reality (Hoos, 1972).

The assumption of universality permits reasoning by deduction even when the research method purports to be inductive. The fitting of local data to a general model requires interpreting the data out of the context in which they were generated. The meaning imposed on them is the understanding of the analyst and not that of the people who produced the data nor of those who will act on them (Braybrooke and Lindblom, 1971).

The problem of separation of the analyst from his or her clients is described by DeLeon (1992):

How can the insulated analyst in Washington know what the recipient in (say) Santa Fe wants, especially if the analyst and the recipient live in and represent vastly different cultures? According to this complaint it is little wonder that the analyst consistently makes recommendations that the recipient finds oddly inadequate or inappropriate; as a consequence the program flounders and often flunks. (1992, 125)

DeLeon goes on to detail how this separation erects barriers to the realization of participatory democracy. This theme is taken up also by Kelly and Maynard-Moody (1993), who blame distancing of analysts from the stakeholders they are to serve on excessive reliance and on positivist and Popperian methodology (see Chapter 5).

Real decision makers do not behave according to the rationalist assumptions of decision theory and policy analysis. Actual observation by March and Simon (1958) of decision makers ended with their rejection of the rational model. Most problems are not well defined and decision makers cannot always order their preferences for consequences of action. The process of decision making, they argued, is more like pulling answers out of a garbage can into which all sorts of information has been thrown. Allison (1971), in his analysis of the process involved in resolving the Cuban missile conflict, offers two other models—bureaucratic and political—of decision making that better fit the data of that series of events. Benveniste (1991) argues that planning and the decision making that it involves is necessarily political. The change of systems requires the exercise of power.

EXPERIENCES WITH NETWORKING AS A MEANS TO DISSEMINATE DATA AND INFORMATION

A networking approach to informing education policy assumes that relevant research findings are available or can be generated and that policy makers are disposed and able to act on those findings.

Those who decide includes not only government officials in the countries, but also employees of bilateral and international assistance agencies and foundations that assist and sometimes encourage countries in the adoption of particular policies. An important objective of education research and policy networks has been to increase exchange of information between members of the various groups, for example, between university-based researchers and World Bank task managers or between researchers and policy makers in a ministry. Researchers were considered to have answers for critical problems in education. On the other hand, policy makers were presumed to be able to define the problems for which they were seeking answers.

Networks are as old as human civilization, but formal attention to networks for education policy began in the late 1950s. For example, the International Development Research Centre of Canada funded the creation of education Northern Research Review and Advisory Groups (NORRAGs) that would compile existing research, commission new research, and seek to disseminate research to policy makers.

NORRAG members, like other networkers before them, began with a view of the informing process as one of transmission of messages from a sender to a receiver, similar to that described previously in this chapter. Over time, several different approaches to networking evolved based on discussions between researchers and policy makers.

Conversations with policy makers about their use of research made it possible to learn for education what C. P. Snow had shown for the physical sciences. Snow (1959) argued that science had relatively little impact on policy because scientists and politicians live in different worlds with different values, language, and interests. Only by reducing those differences can science be utilized more fully. Shaeffer and Nkinyangi (1983) provided many examples of how lack of communication limits use of education research in policy making.

Experiences with Networking in Latin America

One of the most effective networks in education research began about twenty-five years ago in Latin America as an attempt to make results of unpublished research available to scholars and to policy makers. Today the network, called REDUC (Red Latinoamericana de Informacion y Documentacion en Educacion), includes twenty-six research centers in eighteen countries. The centers produce abstracts of mostly unpublished research and education documents. The abstracts are put on microfiche and on a CD-ROM with a software program that permits searching all the documents. The current collection of abstracts covers 28,000 documents.

REDUC's problem has been how to make use of this enormous resource. Various strategies have been tried, including the following:

1. Decision makers invited to meetings and conferences
2. State-of-the-art reviews written about current policy issues

3. Production of brief summaries, or policy briefs, that summarize in nontechnical language what we know about problems and ways to resolve them
4. Training programs for researchers, educators, and policy makers, often together

Cariola (1996) concludes that all these efforts have had some effect but less than a desired one. He is more impressed with the impact on education policy of newcomers to the field, professionals from other disciplines who have not been part of previous efforts at networking. Major policies in education are now taken on the basis of research by economists outside the mainstream of education research.

Cariola sees this crossing of lines as favorable for education. Economists and managers from the business sector bring into education new perspectives that can regenerate creativity in education research and lead to solutions to problems that previously had puzzled us. He cites several examples of the intervention of the newcomers.

At the same time, Cariola argues, there is also increasing attention to a new perspective on knowledge. He distinguishes between knowledge presented as fact, knowledge generated in the process of activity and representational knowledge as knowledge-as-skill. This distinction suggests the value of linking conventional researchers with managers and practitioners to increase our understanding of processes in education.

Cariola summarizes lessons learned from REDUC's experience of attempting to increase utilization of scientific knowledge by decision makers. Among the conclusions he draws are the following:

1. It is not hard to build a database of educational research. The main requirements are a stable institution and a dedicated documentalist.
2. Decision makers do not seek the kind of data researchers can present them. They do not read and they may not understand the forms of presentation used by researchers to communicate to each other.
3. Decision makers do use information. They rely on trusted advisors who are both knowledgeable and who also speak the language of the decision maker.

Cariola also thinks that new technologies of communication may increase use of information by decision makers. This is more likely to the extent that technology presents information in familiar and accessible ways.

Experiences with Networking in Africa

Efforts to develop networks that link researchers and policy makers have been less successful in Africa than in Latin America. The model of networking transferred from the northern RRAG experience has not been appropriate in some African countries. African researchers lack the basic infrastructure required for the level of frequency of communication that sustains a network. It is hard enough to get research done, let alone find the means to share it with other researchers and policy makers.

But this is more a problem at the individual level than at the institutional level. Some institutions have been successful in developing and maintaining networks. The northern RRAG model brings together autonomous individuals, not institutional representatives. In Africa political and economic constraints make this a less effective option than linking institutions together. The institutions in question are primarily state-funded universities. In Africa it might be that development of communication networks will proceed best by working with state institutions rather than associations of private individuals.

In addition to economic and technological constraints, communication in many countries in Africa has suffered from political structures that discourage the free flow of information. Even more difficult are traditions that structure communication by the age and social status of individuals. Exaggerated standards of methodological rigor limit who can be trusted as a communicant. All these factors have most impact when networks are organized as associations of individuals.

Not all experiences have been negative. The Education Research Network for Eastern and Southern Africa (ERNESA) has continued in existence for nine years, encouraging research, communication between researchers and policy makers, and formation of linkages with networks outside the region. The twelve countries in the region are highly disparate in terms of colonial experience, current political structure, economic performance, and cultural traditions. Almost all of them operate with severely constrained resources. The network appears to survive because of the highly felt need for communication, deeply rooted in cultural traditions of mutual aid which are not too different than those in other regions of the world. Perhaps the telling factor in the ERNESA case is the high commitment to education in all the countries of the region. In some cases, this commitment is at the institutional level and in other cases at the individual level. Both contribute to networking.

In South Africa the most important networks in education were organized in opposition to the apartheid government's policies. Some of these, like EduSource in Johannesburg, are funded by independent foundations. University-based networks emerged only with the first steps in 1990 to move toward a democratic society.

Carton (1996) reports on the experience of French-speaking West Africa in order to answer these questions: Can networks develop when the state is weak? and, Are institutions alternative homes for networks? He argues that the African state is more like a rhizome, with multiple centers each capable of growth, than like a root system, with a strong central core. The organization of the state as a collection of factions makes it difficult to keep associations of professionals and the networks they may develop out of the political process. If true, then networks in Africa can be expected to have more impact on policy than in other societies in which there is a clearer distinction between state and civil society.

POLICY DIALOGUE AS PERSUASION

When policy analysts believe that they have the truth, the task of informing policy making becomes one of persuading policy makers to accept the conclusions drawn from the analysis. The analyst is required to abandon his or her neutral, disinterested stance as an objective observer and interpreter of reality and to intervene in the decision process.

The acceptability of this kind of action has increased in recent years, particularly with the ascendancy of supranational agencies in the field of development. Conventional definitions of sovereignty or domain of authority have been set aside as foreign lenders and donors insist that certain conditions be met by the government seeking funding.

An early justification for this kind of intervention is found in Bell (1974) who argued that planners (meaning those working for the international assistance agencies) can be most effective in situations in which "the government is perceived neither by itself nor by others as a custodian of that difficult and ambiguous concept, the national interest. Rather it is an 'operational' alliance between various interest groups which aim to grasp and preserve power, which also needs to be continuously cemented and possibly extended" (Bell, 1974, 70).

The process has been called policy dialogue especially by supranational agencies engaged in requiring national governments to make structural adjustments in their economies and political structures. There has been no systematic treatment of the practice of policy dialogue or its effects on the content and effectiveness of educational plans. We should be careful to distinguish between instances of genuine dialogue, in which outcomes cannot be predicted from either set of planners' objectives, to instances of political manipulation, in which the powerful impose their plans based on rational planning. Observers of the structural adjustment process sometimes argue that there has been little actual dialogue, primarily because the actors in the conversation do not have equal amounts of power nor begin with shared values (Mayer, 1990).

The following set of requisite conditions for dialogue is consistent with the definition of the process as one-way persuasion:

1. The issue must be of concern to the decision maker.
2. There must be counterparts for the external actor. Someone in the policy maker's group has to serve as a broker or go-between with the researcher.
3. The decision maker must be predisposed to use research-based information.[1]
4. The focus must not be on research. The ultimate aim of the process is dialogue and marketing.
5. Mere dissemination is not sufficient. "The marketing of policy change must be technically very proficient [in order to overcome expected political opposition to the change proposed by new policy]. The key interest groups must be identified, and the 'buttons' that motivate them must be pushed. . . . Researchers must be able to handle both the communications aspects and the research/political economy aspects" (Crouch, 1993, 5).

The purpose of this process is to convince policy makers to act as the researchers would have them act. Researchers engage in

A process of marketing, as opposed to design, of the policy reform. To put it crudely, it is a highly sophisticated, carefully crafted sales job that creates the feeling of inclusiveness and co-ownership of the reform process. The best situation is if such a process in fact is inclusive and is in fact co-owned by all the stake-holders, as long as the consultative nature does not extend to the basic choices but creates ownership of the decisions after the fact. (Crouch, 1993, 10)

The sales job is easier when the pronouncements of the analysts are seen as being based on an objective reading of the facts and their arguments as being unquestionable and untainted by mere political considerations. Four ways in which policy analysts can manipulate information are the following:

1. Deliberately using technical jargon and sophisticated analyses to obfuscate issues
2. Appealing to openness and dependence on experts to create false assurance
3. Arguing that a political issue is actually a technical issue
4. Holding back information about other alternatives, misrepresenting the validity of analyses, and claiming success for untested options (Forester, 1989)

Only after several years of experience has it been noted that benefit–cost analysis, like rational planning, requires information seldom available except in the most routine situations. Analysts make subjective judgments but pass them off as objective (Downs and Larkey, 1986). Political objectives rather than objective analysis often determine which issues were considered important (Whittington and Macrae, 1986).

NOTE

1. The language of Crouch is a bit more formal. He argues that "there must be some space for technocracy," and that "human rights, peace negotiations, etc., typically, therefore, are not productive fields for a policy dialogue approach" (1993, 4).

Chapter 5

Utilization Stimulated by Providing Decision Makers with Data

The approaches to utilization of knowledge discussed in Chapter 4 emphasize the interests of the knowledge producer, who is not the ultimate knowledge user. In this chapter we describe several alternative approaches. The major distinction between these alternatives and the methods described in Chapter 4 is that the alternatives give priority to the interests of the policy maker rather than to the knowledge producer. The approaches described in Chapter 4 are based on the assumption that the expert is more qualified than the policy maker to determine which information is of greatest value. The approaches described in this chapter assume that the policy maker is at least as capable as the expert of identifying which information is of most importance.

This competence of the policy maker has at least two bases. The first is that the knowledge that is important in policy making includes the values and goals of the policy maker and his or her constituents. Policy makers have much better and often exclusive access to this kind of knowledge. The second is that policy makers are more likely to have that kind of knowledge, derived from experience, which is essential to determine the political viability of technically defined policy options. Experts may know more about whether A is related to B, but the policy maker knows most about whether it is B or C that is desired, and knows more about the political costs of pursuing various kinds of actions to achieve *B* or *C*.

We have ordered the sequence of alternative approaches to reflect, more or less, the amount of knowledge that is presumed to be generated or compiled by the expert. All the approaches call for participation by those who will utilize the knowledge. In the approaches first presented, the only knowledge that is explicitly recognized comes from the experts. In the latter approaches there is specific attention to the kind of knowledge contributed by decision makers. The sequence is of approaches that emphasize dissemination as a process controlled by the expert to approaches that emphasize dialogue, in which there is an exchange between all participants.

PROBLEMS OF DISSEMINATION

The dissemination of research findings in order to inform policy is problematic because of the differences between how researchers and policy makers think. At best, dissemination will contribute to enlightening the choices made, but given the different worlds of research and policy makers, it is hard to engineer impact of this type of knowledge on decisions. "It is one thing to say that we can find examples of research having an impact on policy, and of how research 'percolates' or enlightens or indirectly raises consciousness. But it is another thing to assume that impacts can be engineered" (Husen and Kogan, 1984, 78).

Weiss (1979) has characterized alternative models to examine the relationship between research and policy. She concludes that the linear model, in which policy development is assumed to follow research on the topics addressed by policy, provides an inadequate characterization of the links between research and policy in the public policy domain. Husen and Kogan (1984), upon reviewing experiences on the links between research and policy in a number of countries, concur with this assessment. There must be a policy orientation in the analysis and in the dialogue surrounding the analysis in order for research to illuminate immediate policy questions.

In order to more directly serve as a foundation for policy, research-based knowledge should have the following characteristics:

1. An interdisciplinary approach to analyze public policies that emulates the way in which decision makers perceive their problems. "Real decisions, as we all know, do not respect the boundaries of the academic disciplines: they always have political, economic, and organizational components; they may well also have legal, educational, biological, or other technical implications as well" (Trow, 1994).

2. A policy orientation in the analysis. That means that the purpose of the analysis is not just to understand the conditions bearing on a particular problem but to inform decisions which can influence those conditions. In practice this approach leads to maximizing the role of factors which can be influenced by policy and to minimize the role of those which cannot. An understanding of the feasibility of options to address certain problems (political, financial, or organizational) is central to policy analysis and distinguishes it from most academic research.

3. An emphasis on understanding the problem from the perspective of the client (the decision maker) who attempts to influence conditions bearing on the problem. This means recognizing the degrees of freedom of the decision maker and emphasizing those conditions and variables which are more readily affected by the policies falling under his or her authority.

4. An emphasis on conducting the analysis within the time limits of the policy cycle and other resource constraints. Academic researchers are less concerned with completion deadlines than are policy analysts. The policy analyst is particularly aware of the importance of opportunity to influence decisions. The distinguishing feature of much analysis for decisions is that it has to be timely and relevant to the issues at hand.

Most education research conducted in academic institutions does not have these characteristics. It is not surprising, therefore, that the ambition to make policy fit research-based knowledge often is frustrated.

EXPERIENCES IN DATA AND INFORMATION DISSEMINATION

Given that policy makers and researchers live in separate cultures, what can bring them together? How can policy makers become aware of the information generated by research? We describe five approaches to help answer these questions.

The Knowledge Broker

Some have proposed that in order for research-based knowledge to serve policy a knowledge broker is necessary, someone who can link the worlds of research and analysis and policy (Kogan, Konnan, and Henkel, 1980). A similar concept has been proposed under the more general term of expert in a study on social science research utilization for public policy in Finland:

What is usually needed when shifting from the domain of research to the realm of politics is a transformation process, in which research results are evaluated and translated into practical recommendations. This is usually done by others than researchers, for instance by politicians, administrators, interest group activists, or journalists. If researchers take part in the transformation process, they adapt themselves to an expert role in which they do not only present the consequences of some actions but give also values to the policy alternatives. . . . The expert does not substitute the politician or any other-decision maker. He brings his actual knowledge and value judgments to the decision-making process and thus provides one alternative for designing the decision. . . . The task of the expert is to convert scientific findings to policy recommendations, but the conversion of advice into decisions remains the domain of decision-makers. (Lampinen, 1992)

Policy analysts or experts can work as brokers between the worlds of research and the worlds of policy. Husen (1984), however, incorporates them into the same category of policy makers:

The last group [policy analysts] rather quickly tends to become socialized into the orientations and opinions prevailing among administrators and/or policy makers in the Ministry. . . . However, professionals with research background in ministries or central agencies represent a new and proliferating species. . . . As a distinct category with a particular type of training they are as yet mainly to be found in America. (8)

Various authors have pointed out how the links between research and policy are strengthened as the boundaries between each professional field become blurred. At a symposium on the links between research and policy, participants from Sweden indicated how researchers oftentimes work as administrators and policy makers and how policy makers themselves conduct some education research activities. "Sweden, together with the USA, is an example of the maximum interaction of policy and research, although the two countries are very different in context and therefore in the ways in which research findings and speculations enter the policy bloodstream" (Husen and Kogan, 1984, 49).

The linkages between researchers and policy makers take different forms. Ad hoc commissions have been appointed by the Cabinet in Sweden and other countries to prepare policy analyses. In many cases social scientists have formed part of these commissions. In Germany, "the Education Commission of the German Educational Council included experts in educational research, scientists with general interest in education and representatives from public life" (Husen and Kogan, 1984, 9). In Finland university professors or researchers have traditionally been appointed in ad hoc committees to advise Parliament, which has requested official comments from universities and appointed researchers as experts in parliamentary committees (Lampinen, 1992). In the United States, the influence of policy analysis is more direct in the Executive Branch than in the legislative. A study of the use of analysis by Congressional staff found that even though staff paid attention to evidence, it rarely shaped policy directions. Analysis had a very limited enlightenment function for Congress and had minor impact on the substance of legislative action:

Congressional committee staff were clear that analysis doesn't have a chance of setting broad direction for public policy. Setting political direction is what members of Congress are elected to do and what staff are hired to help them do. Meeting the needs of constituents, mediating the interests of lobbies and groups, following the ideological proclivities that got them elected in the first place—that is the member's role. (Weiss, 1989, 428)

With the appropriate mediation of a broker or expert, research-based information or processed and interpreted data from research studies are potentially of great use to decision makers. The volume of research studies that report analyses of data is, however, enormous. Computerized databases, such as Micro-ISIS, ERIC, the REDUC system of Latin America, and the SEABAS system of Southeast Asia, maintain a large number of research reports. The UNESCO series on educational innovations includes a lot of information based on research, as do publications of the Regional Information Network of INNOTECH in the Philippines.[1] The Iberoamerican Office of Education produces a series of comparative reports on education systems in a computer-readable laser disk. UNESCO's International Bureau of Education also publishes a computer-readable laser disk with World Data on Education, including descriptions and basic statistics of evaluation systems around the world. The World Bank publishes a computer-readable laser disk with educational statistics (Stars) for all countries in the world. There are many government and commercial journals that publish results of education research. Also, research information is generated on a regular basis in almost every country in the form of master's and occasional doctoral theses.

This enormous volume of information has little direct effect on policy. Research-based information in individual studies, including those generated locally, is seldom if ever consulted by decision makers or policy makers. In addition to problems of physical as well as conceptual accessibility, the sheer volume discourages all but the most serious scholar or the diligent research assistant.

Syntheses of Education Research

A number of efforts have been made to synthesize research-based information to make it more accessible and useful to decision makers. The simplest efforts categorize studies in terms of whether they confirm that a particular policy (or intervention) has a positive effect. One of the most cited of this version of research report is that by Fuller (1987), who synthesized research on factors associated with higher levels of student achievement reported in 185 studies. Study results were assigned a plus, zero, or minus to indicate the direction of the relationship between achievement and the various factors. The text encourages readers to believe that the best policies for raising levels of achievement are those that had the highest proportion of pluses. Fuller's approach was expanded by Loera (1988), working for the Harvard University BRIDGES project,[2] who reviewed more than 400 studies and organized them into a computerized database that would respond to queries about policies to improve levels of achievement.

Both efforts have been used in workshops to train decision makers in the use of research for policy making. The reactions have been disappointing. The decision makers focus on the minority negative findings and want to know about the contextual variables that probably explain their appearance. They report that the extensive collection of findings is not interesting, even when presented on a computer screen. Some decision makers note that the lists of findings are like answers to questions they have not asked. Instead, they want to know what are the important questions they should ask.

Perhaps the best known efforts to synthesize research findings are the state-of-the-art research reviews encouraged by the International Development Research Centre of Canada and later by the RRAGs that the IDRC financed. Reviews of this kind have also been produced under the sponsorship of the World Bank, USAID, SIDA, GTZ, and other agencies. A dozen were produced under the BRIDGES project.

Many of these reviews differ from ordinary reviews of research literature found in academic journals. They include studies that would not make it into academic journals because of limited sample size or weak statistical analysis, and they focus explicitly on specifying what works from a policy perspective, rather than on hypothesis testing. In addition to reviews focusing on single policy issues, there are book-length syntheses of research (Chapman and Carrier, 1990; Hopkins, 1989; Lockheed and Verspoor, 1991; Psacharopolous and Woodhall, 1985; United States Agency for International Development, 1990).

Several informal efforts to evaluate the usefulness of state-of-the-art reviews and book-length syntheses indicate that while they are highly valued by researchers, especially those in poor countries that do not otherwise have access to research studies and results, they seldom are read by policy makers. The major complaints are that they are too long, too esoteric, and not concrete enough to respond to the problem of a particular decision maker. This observation also holds for book-length publications summarizing research and, of course, for encyclopedias. However, the informal studies also indicate that the long-term impact of these reviews on policy can be high. In many countries, the reviews are primary reading material in teacher training institutions and university education faculties. The next generation of teachers and decision makers will have been informed by this method of communication.

Other efforts to share results of research with decision makers have organized access to research results using a framework which attempts to reflect policy choices or the kinds of questions which decision makers need to answer to formulate policy. SHARE is a policy-structured database which provides access to about 1,000 summaries of research reports in developing countries to support education policy. It was developed at HIID under the USAID-funded ABEL project. HIID has recently published a book, following a nonlinear format of presentation, to introduce research-based information step-by-step by following a series of questions from decision makers (McGinn and Borden, 1995). As part of the ABEL project, HIID also published *The Forum*, a magazine designed to disseminate results of research and evaluation to education decision makers and practitioners organizing information under common policy topics.

Training in Use of Research

A third approach to share results of research with decision makers has been through training programs. The interaction between trainer and decision maker makes it possible to organize information of immediate importance, and to present that information within a conceptual framework that enables the decision maker to formulate questions of the research-based data. However, training programs are limited in time and highly expensive. Furthermore, there are no published studies that evaluate the impact of this training on use of research information in decision making.

Networking As a Means to Disseminate Data and Information

McGinn (1996) reviews the experiences of twenty-five networks designed to link education researchers across continents and to link researchers with policy makers and with international assistance agencies. The networks were organized by different groups, namely, governments, UNESCO, universities, and associations of education research centers. All the networks were intended to increase utilization of research-based information in education policy making in developing countries.

The emphasis in this work is on networking, rather than on the technical aspects of the networks or their databases. Networking is seen as a process that taps the knowledge, as opposed to data, held by persons and institutions. The personal quality of the knowledge that is gained is considered to be a positive attribute.

Information derived from databases, whether about individuals or about themes and issues in the literature, does not make value judgments about the persons concerned or the quality of the article, report, or book. The consultant database will not reveal whether the individual is a good colleague or team member. . . . For a busy decision maker, access to a database that will provide twenty abstracts from different journals about class size or about quality issues in vocational training is really of little help. . . . The database will not say that one single piece on that topic is better than the other nineteen put together . . . but this is what policy makers require. (King, 1996, 19–20)

Networking contributes to institutional capacity by virtue of developing relationships of trust that encourage further sharing of information and, eventually, development of consensus about institutional goals. Most networks are secondary organizations. They are relatively temporary and voluntary associations of persons who hold primary allegiance to other organizations. The culture of the primary organization may be contradictory to the values required for networking. For example, a scientific organization may discourage personal relationships in which objectivity is not a primary value. The more successful the network, in terms of exchange of personal knowledge and development of shared values, the more conflict with the primary organization.

Networks can be made up of individuals or institutions. In societies and organizations characterized by a relatively high tolerance for individualism, autonomous individuals can participate in networks without too much concern about losing their place in their primary organization. In other societies and organizations in which community or collective values take precedence, networking must be carried out through institutional channels. A classic model for networking is the university. Individual faculty members are allowed to participate in any kind of network on the assumption that the free pursuit of the truth eventually will benefit the university as a community of scholars. In some societies universities are not autonomous from the state, or from private owners. Information is seen as a valuable, and scarce, commodity; its free flow is discouraged rather than encouraged. When they are created, networks link institutions with each other rather than individuals.

The use of networking as a means of spreading or sharing information must, therefore, be adjusted to the values dominant in the particular situation. Networks in Africa modeled after those successful in the United States and Europe have had little success (McGinn, 1996). The European and U.S. networks brought individuals together as unofficial representatives of their organizations. The network members develop new knowledge which is then taken back to their primary organizations. In Africa, however, network members are more successful when they are official representatives of their institutions. The consensus that eventually is developed is institutional rather than personal. This process requires more time and resources; therefore, most of these networks die. If they were to survive, however, they would have more impact on policy than would networks made up of individuals who act independently of their primary organizations.

Networks of researchers have had little impact on education policy in developing countries, although they have developed an impressive body of shared research knowledge. These networks have not yet developed a strategy for active involvement of decision makers.

It is one thing to collect and make information available. It is a very different thing to dish it out in a way that is useful to decision makers in their every day practice. It is unusual for decision makers to use "fresh" knowledge in their practice. In this business, therefore, you have to work more on the demand side than on the supply side. The real challenge in the use of knowledge is not technical, organizational, or financial. It is cultural. (Cariola, 1996, 155)

Perhaps because most networks are organized by university-based researchers, the networking approach to knowledge utilization continues to reflect the culture of the expert rather than the culture of the decision maker. Although the rhetoric of networking favors dialogue, the practice of it is not yet achieved.

DATA COLLECTION METHODS USED
TO STIMULATE DIALOGUE

There are three methods used to move beyond a simple dissemination of data and information to a discussion or dialogue with policy makers. The methods maintain the privileged status of the researcher as expert in techniques of research, but they do take steps toward engaging the researcher in a discussion with the policy maker about the meaning of the information provided.

Management Information Systems

In addition to information based on national and comparative research, ministries of education generally collect educational statistics
and other data that can be used to inform policy. Data by themselves are not information, but the analysis of policy options can be
informed by the appropriate analysis of existing educational data.

During the 1980s, a growing emphasis developed in management
information systems on the assumption that education managers
often lacked basic facts about the education systems of which they
were in charge (Chapman and Mahlck, 1993). This was stimulated
by the growing pressures on international development agencies to
demonstrate the impact of their education projects.

Cassidy (1996) has developed a framework to organize information system interventions. He identifies the following fifteen key
steps in information system construction:

1. specification of information needs
2. prioritization
3. integration
4. synchronization
5. organization and design
6. computerization
7. data collection and gathering
8. verifications and followup
9. data entry
10. validation
11. data cleaning
12. storage and maintenance
13. dissemination and access
14. denial and reconciliation
15. utilization

Cutting across all these steps, he proposes that there are technical
issues, training issues, organizational issues (pertaining to the ministry of education), and institutional issues (pertaining to the larger
public sector). In Cassidy's view most information development efforts have focused only on technical issues and training issues, and
only on the more technical steps of system organization and design, computerization, data collection and gathering, verification
and followup, data entry, validation, data cleaning, and storage and
maintenance. Cassidy's view is that sustainable information system

development is not only a technical issue but an organizational, social, and political issue. Most interventions in this area neglect the latter three dimensions.

The development of relational database software, of applications for statistical analysis, and of packages for geographical display of data in off-the-shelf and low-cost packages, and the rapid development of information technologies to store, process, and retrieve large volumes of data at declining costs further expanded the possibility of developing systems of education statistics and indicator systems to support management and decision making.

Information system interventions can be classified by how many data are analyzed, interpreted, and organized into information. In some cases, information systems have been used to process educational statistics on enrollment, repetition, promotion, and personnel and physical resources. This represents the most basic level of the use of modern computer technology and software to store and retrieve traditional educational information. In other cases, systems have been developed to monitor student achievement. A higher level of value added is represented by the integration of multiple databases, for example, data on student achievement, regular education statistics, information from the census or household surveys, and so on. In other cases, indicator systems have been developed to monitor project implementation and impact on project targets. In a few cases, information systems have been used to investigate relationships between outcomes, for example, student achievement, repetition, and educational inputs and processes.

The most rare instances are those in which information systems have been used at the highest levels of value added, for instance, integrating information on student achievement with other databases which permit the examination of relationships between factors. But even at the lowest level of adding value to these data, a significant impact in policy design occurs when information systems are used to order and present existing statistics. Given our earlier discussion of education organizations as being poorly integrated both horizontally and vertically, it should not be surprising that the effective presentation of data to decision makers can improve the focus and appropriateness of policies.

In 1991, HIID conducted a study in Honduras on the reasons why children repeated grades in rural primary schools. One of the factors identified as having a strong influence on repetition was single-teacher schools, where poorly trained teachers had a hard time creating opportunities for children in four or five different grades to learn. Using official statistics on number of teachers per school and a geographically referenced relational software, we were able to show the regions of the country with the most single-teacher schools. The discussions of the findings of this study, along with the geographic information system which highlighted the regions with predominantly single-teacher schools, led Honduran policy makers to provide guidelines for new teacher appointments in these areas.

In the preparation of a strategic education plan in Paraguay in 1996, an HIID team processed existing information in the statistical system of the planning unit of the Ministry of Education to show the number of schools with one teacher, two teachers, three teachers, and so on. This information had never been presented in the statistical yearbook and regular publications of the ministry. The high proportion of schools which operated with less than three teachers surprised many senior ministry staff—initially some claimed that there was probably some mistake in how the information had been processed—as well as most of the representatives of civil society and various groups who participated in discussions of the plan.

In Malawi, an HIID consultant assisting in the development of the educational statistical system in 1993 suggested creating a table displaying student–teacher ratios by standard (grade). The wide disparities in these ratios, which were four times as high for first grade as for the upper grades, again surprised senior decision makers.

In El Salvador, as part of the preparation of an education sector assessment conducted in 1993, an HIID team used data from the census to prepare a table displaying the percentage of children from different income groups who were out of school at different ages. This table showed that 15 percent of the children never entered school, and that for the poorest 20 percent of the population, one in four children never entered school, and that the poorer children entered school later and stayed there less years than the children from higher socioeconomic groups.

Information systems have been used to inform policies providing factual evidence to ground the discussions and the exploration of options. That the simple presentation of data can have such a dramatic effect toward enlightening the policy discussions only reinforces the inadequate factual foundation of much policy making. Of course, data do not speak for themselves, but the direct incorporation of data in policy discussions helps to provide some basic empirical evidence to the problems which are discussed and permits the separation of facts from inferences people make about the facts. It is then possible to reach agreement over preferred courses of action at low levels of inference. For instance, in El Salvador, all those discussing the discrepancies in access for children from different socioeconomic backgrounds agreed in recognizing this as a problem and a priority for action, albeit for different reasons.

Survey Research and Consultation Procedures

Some education problems require a more focused base of information than is provided by information systems based on annual school statistics. Information systems are of limited use as the information required to shape policy moves from description to analysis and explanation. The analysis which can be done by examining relationships with basic statistics is limited and does not take into account the role of mediating or intervening factors. For example, even in systems which measure student achievement or some other learning outcome, it is rare to find adequate measures of social class. This has a direct effect on learning outcomes and interacts with school practices.

One way to resolve this problem is to design surveys to identify critical factors that influence learning. For instance, in trying to understand the reasons for repetition in Honduras, an HIID team designed a sample survey that examined the contribution of school and out-of-school factors to repetition. Surveys can also have a broader scope. They make it possible to assess the relative importance of ways to improve student achievement. When combined with information about the costs of these interventions, survey data can provide a solid foundation to assess the relative cost effectiveness of policy options.

We should clarify that not all surveys can inform policy equally. Survey research is a methodology used to collect information from large numbers of informants. It can have multiple purposes. Surveys can be used to compare education systems on a number of comparable indicators or to understand in greater detail a particular education system, with more attention to factors which are specific to that system. Surveys can have a theoretical orientation, interested in testing or developing theories, or they can have a policy orientation, interested in the specific contribution of factors which policy makers in a given sector can influence. For example, during the last couple of decades, the IEA has conducted cross-national surveys aimed at informing a model of school learning. The IEA studies have generally been criticized as having a limited policy impact. Perhaps one reason for this is that these studies were built on the assumption that there is a universal model of school learning and that different countries represented variations over that basic model. Cross-national variation was then used to infer the key elements of the model. Based on this assumption, the emphasis in data collection and analysis was on exploring variation between countries and not variation within countries. However, from the point of view of informing national education policies, within-country variation is of great interest.

In most IEA surveys the school models were built after the information had been collected. There was no formal exercise of model building as a precondition to design data collection instruments and data analysis techniques. Recently, there have been two important changes in the IEA movement. The first is an attempt to test formally a school model designed a priori. The second is an attempt to solve some of the earlier shortcomings in terms of policy impact by formal inclusion of ministries of education in the design of the model.

We have used both types of sample surveys: those aimed at testing a universal model and those designed to construct a local model of school operation useful for policy formulation. The problems associated with informing policy on the basis of this research fall under the category of problems of dissemination.

The design of the policy surveys begins with the client—the user—in mind. They are based more on the fundamentals of program evaluation research than on the classical approach to survey research. Policy-oriented surveys can provide evidence to construct a school model for a specific context. An important part of this information is descriptive, offering more detail about school inputs, practices, and outcomes than is generally the case with the typical systems of statistics routinely collected by ministries. Another part of the knowledge generated by the model is analytic, examining how different variables relate to each other and providing a sense about the dynamics of the school system on the basis of the natural variation of the factors measured and how those interact.

Under the BRIDGES project a number of surveys were conducted in countries to help decision makers understand the factors that most contribute to learning. While the project started with the aim of designing cross-country research that would allow the preparation of a single, universal, school model—along the lines of prior studies of international achievement—it soon recognized that in order to have maximum value to policy makers in specific countries, surveys would have to be tailored to serve specific information needs of these clients.

A survey with these characteristics was carried out in Pakistan in 1988. The survey was developed at the time of the first democratically elected government of Benazir Bhutto, after a decade of military rule. Many of the political decision makers in education recognized they were outsiders to the sector and required basic information to understand how schools worked in the country. The federal Minister of Education had been the principal of an elite private school in Lahore, and she had been educated in private schools and abroad. Communication between those who had responsibility to make the education system respond to the priorities of the new democratic government and the permanent staff of the civil service was less than perfect. We designed a survey that would characterize primary schools in the country, that would provide information on the results of prior attempts to improve education, and that would suggest areas of greatest potential for further improvement.

We initiated the survey by interviewing approximately 100 senior- and mid-level administrators in the federal and provincial ministries. These interviews served to identify main issues of concern to these administrators, as well as to identify past efforts of school improvement. On the basis of this information, as well as a review of prior education research in Pakistan and international literature on the determinants of student achievement, we designed a survey to collect information about the following: student achievement in mathematics and science in grade five; the social and family environment of individual students; and instructional and management practices of teachers and principals. We administered approximately 11,000 tests and interviewed 1,000 teachers and 500 principals. The analysis of these data provided a detailed description of the realities of primary education in Pakistan. We were able to identify the factors which made the greatest difference in levels of student achievement. We sought to understand what had happened with the implementation of several innovations to improve school quality (Warwick, Reimers, and McGinn, 1992; Warwick and Reimers, 1995).

This survey used a BRIDGES project methodology that designed school surveys to inform policy in specific contexts. The methodology involved taking into account the frameworks policy makers and managers use to think about education problems. The surveys then became opportunities to provide support or disconfirm some of the policy makers' beliefs. A similar approach was used in Honduras, where a small survey was conducted to understand the factors which contributed to school repetition. We began the survey work by interviewing decision makers and managers about their theories of repetition. It was then possible to design the survey as a formal test of those theories and to present the results in ways which would start with the frames of reference that decision makers had about repetition.

Surveys can also be used to monitor and modify opinions and beliefs of teachers or other participants in the education system. The objective here is not necessarily to explain a problem (e.g., low levels of achievement or high levels of repetition), but is to understand how key participants in the education process think about these problems or about efforts to improve them. For example, the Ministry of Education in Paraguay conducted a survey in 1996 to obtain opinions and suggestions from teachers participating in a pilot program of bilingual education. The analysis of these results helped the managers of the program understand some of the difficulties experienced in implementation of the program, such as the tardiness in the delivery of textbooks and instructional materials and the perceived deficiency of the training teachers had received. The managers also gained a better understanding of the responses of parents to the program.

Other consultation procedures to solicit the views of different stakeholders of the education process include focus groups, roundtables, and interviews. These methods are especially important if we think of education policy as the result of the beliefs, attitudes, and behaviors of teachers, parents, and others in the education system. In Paraguay, the Ministry of Education conducted a series of focus group interviews with teachers in 1995 to obtain feedback about the implementation of a curriculum reform. Teachers' assessments of the methods used to train them, as well as the recommendation of teachers to have more local-based training, led the ministry to shift the approach used to deliver the new curriculum to the teachers. Delivery was shifted from a centralized, hierarchical system of training by experts to a school-based system of self-training and training at the local level.

Sector Assessments

An education sector assessment is an examination of broad educational problems and constraints with the aim of identifying options for policy reform. The emphasis in a sector assessment is on the examination of linkages between the education system and the broader economic, societal, and political systems of which education is a part, and also on the examination of the specific subsystems of education and how those contribute to the overall performance of the sector. An assessment starts by laying out the goals and objectives of the education sector in a given country, and then answers whether the education system is achieving those goals using multiple methodologies and sources of information. It goes on to examine whether it is achieving those goals by making the best possible use of financial, human, and institutional resources.

Sector assessments are a standard way to obtain a comprehensive diagnosis of an education system. Variations of this methodology have been promoted by development agencies since the 1970s. USAID has conducted sector assessments as a way to initiate dialogue with a host-country government on options for improvement. Sector assessments have served as a source of baseline information

on the education system of the country and for the design of education projects. In the early 1980s, a major USAID project called Improving the Efficiency of Educational Systems (IEES) and based at
Florida State University refined this methodology as a strategy to
improve the capacity of governments to make better education policies (Pigozzi and Cieutat, 1988) and carried out numerous sector
assessments around the world (IEES, 1986, 1988a, 1988b). The IEES
manual defines a sector assessment as the following:

A detailed analysis of the goals and objectives, status, plans, needs, constraints, and priority target areas with rank ordered recommendations for
actions in a national education system. The methodology set forth in this
manual is based on a systems approach to education. Thus, all components
of the sector are analyzed interdependently, in relation to one another, and
in relation to the broader context, especially the overriding economic conditions and the existing capacity to manage educational activities. Objectives of the assessment are to encourage the use of relevant and current
information for planning, policy formulation, and resource allocation that
will improve efficiency throughout the entire education sector. This is very
different from evaluation, which is an appraisal to determine the significance or value of a single activity or set of activities.

A subsector assessment is the description and analysis of a component (i.e.,
subsector) in the education sector. For example, subsector assessments might
address primary, secondary, vocational, higher, or nonformal education.
The integration, analysis, and synthesis of all subsector assessments com-
prises a sector assessment. (Pigozzi and Cieutat, 1988, 3)

The World Bank and regional development banks also carry out
sector assessments at the early stages of discussions with governments aimed at preparing education loans. A World Bank manual
defines the purpose of sector assessment as the following:

[Sector assessment is] concerned with the examination and analysis of a
country's development problems, policies, institutions, and investment
priorities. It has three primary objectives. The first is to provide a thorough
knowledge of trends and government policies in the sector. The second is
to identify significant problems, including current government policies, that
affect the development of education. The third is to evaluate, on the basis
of sound analytical diagnosis, policy options that could improve the contribution of education to economic growth and societal welfare. (Mingat
and Tang, 1988, 1)

Our interest in sector assessments is twofold. As complex data
collection efforts, they permit the construction of a systemic view
of education. This systemic view has much more of a chance of
stimulating the interest of policy makers than does research which

focuses on a single issue. Also, the process of the sector assessment requires contact with policy makers and officials at various levels.

Data Collection. As a methodology or as a combination of methodologies to examine broad issues of effectiveness, efficiency, and equity in education, sector assessments emphasize the generation of technical knowledge as a foundation to define education policies. Sector assessments are an approach, much as policy-oriented surveys or as research in general, to generate knowledge which can inform decision making. They are another type of rational inquiry to better understand education systems and to plan actions to change them.

The process of conducting a sector assessment is defined as a technical process for generating objective knowledge. The aim is to produce knowledge that is based on evidence and processed using standard methodologies which allow one to draw conclusions subject to verification by independent analysts. For example, the IEES manual identifies the following major steps in a sector assessment: preparation of terms of reference of resources and team, data collection, data analysis, identification of issues and constraints, conclusions, recommendations, review, and revision (Pigozzi and Cieutat, 1988).

The outline of a typical sector assessment will examine the various subsystems of education (i.e., primary, secondary, vocational, nonformal, higher, and teacher education), the subsystems of specific interest in a particular country (i.e., early childhood education, special education, firm-based training, and graduate education), and the political, social, and economic contexts and issues of sector finance and management. Also, there may be special chapters for issues of particular interest in the country, such as interdonor coordination, religious education, private education, curriculum, or assessments of major government initiatives in education. For each of these subsystems, a typical chapter will cover a description of the status (i.e., goals, strategies, structures, and programs), will include an analysis of needs, plans, constrains, and major issues of external and internal efficiency, equity, management, and financing, and will conclude by proposing recommendations.

In the preparation of a sector assessment, efforts are made to cover as much information as possible about the sector. The sources of information include existing statistics and program records, interviews with key informants, observations of schools and training sites, and review of existing research and pertinent literature. Occasionally, quick surveys are conducted to fill in gaps. With this information, the preparation of an assessment using the framework outlined becomes similar to trying to put together a puzzle. Assessments become major reference documents for further work and policy reform in the sector.

The methodologies used to analyze existing data or additional data occasionally collected for specific purposes include demographic analysis, enrollment projections, cost analysis, rate-of-return analysis, analysis of equity disparities, analysis of organizational constraints, and examination of the soundness and consistency in pedagogical approaches used in interdependent subsystems (e.g., curriculum taught at different levels and teacher training). Though the broad and comprehensive focus of an assessment makes it distinct from a program evaluation, there is much similarity between the way evaluators collect and process evidence and the work of professionals conducting sector assessments. Both will combine extensive qualitative interviewing with quantitative analysis of pertinent data and with document analysis and site visits. An important distinction is that sector assessments are more open ended in scope and lack the focus provided in the evaluation of a specific program or policy. A sector assessment is as interested in understanding the performance of the education system in terms of what is being done as it is in terms of what is not being done. Good sector assessments are equally likely to highlight successful strategies as they are to point out windows of opportunities for future strategies.

The preparation of a sector assessment varies in scope from a few weeks to several months. An assessment conducted by the IEES team in Haiti, for instance, required 292 person days, while another assessment sponsored by the same organization in Indonesia required 848 person days (Pigozzi and Cieutat, 1988). HIID conducted an education sector assessment in El Salvador in 1993. The preparation of the assessment was structured in the following nine subprojects:

1. Economic analysis and implications for education
2. Costs
3. Benefits and financing of education
4. Basic and early childhood education
5. Secondary education
6. Technical and vocational education
7. Higher education
8. Nonformal education
9. Management training and management and decentralization of education

Different teams were in charge of each of these projects and each produced a report which became a chapter in the sector assessment. The final report was a 640-page book with an introductory summary chapter and a chapter for each of these themes (Reimers, 1995).

Communication with Policy Makers. The nature of the information sought in a sector assessment requires communication with decision makers. For instance, the team in El Salvador working in economic analysis had extensive meetings with senior staff in the ministry of finance, central bank, and planning ministry. They examined all reports and official figures and forecasts about the macroeconomic conditions. Upon identifying the most dynamic sectors of the economy—export-oriented industry—they interviewed chief executive officers (CEOs) of large and medium firms to obtain information about the needs and constrains they perceived in the training of the labor force. They also conducted analyses of data obtained in the household survey and in several censuses to examine the relationships between education, employment, and productivity. This team developed a model that forecast education and training needs of the labor force under several alternative scenarios of growth of the economy. Other analyses compared and discussed the educational level of the labor force in El Salvador with that of other nations that had showed rapid growth during the last decades.

The team working in the chapter of costs and financing of education consulted with ministry staff in the preparation of unit costs at different levels and types of education. Historical and cross-national comparisons were made between the level of effort made by El Salvador financing education as a percentage of GNP, total government expenditures, and total expenditures. The research team obtained information on private contributions to basic and higher education from surveys conducted by the team working on the chapters in basic and higher education. They assessed the percentage of the planned budget which was actually spent by different items and levels of expenditure. This chapter provided recommendations regarding the level and distribution of education expenditures for several scenarios of improvement of access and quality of education.

The team working on basic and early childhood education examined all existing research on the subject in the country, interviewed government officials in charge of various programs, and conducted a survey in a nationally representative sample of approximately 150 primary schools to evaluate the implementation, impact, and views of beneficiaries of various programs, to improve access and quality, and to assess existing conditions in schools. Also, they analyzed dates obtained from the information system of the Ministry of Education with data on enrollments, repetition, and staff. They conducted secondary analysis of data from several household surveys and censuses. The chapter they prepared discussed issues of access, quality, and efficiency of primary education, identified the major problems and the causes for those problems, and proposed avenues for improvement. There was significant emphasis in the preparation of the chapter on two major government initiatives to improve access and quality of primary education.

The team working in secondary education reviewed all existing research and program documentation about the level, carried out secondary analysis of existing statistics about the subsector, interviewed government officials and different administrative levels, and conducted interviews with focus groups of teachers, principals, and students in several regions of the country. The chapter examined the main problems of access, quality, and efficiency and suggested options for improvement of this level.

The team working on technical and vocational education conducted a survey of all public and private institutions providing training at this level and in-depth interviews with administrators, employers, and government institutions. The analysis of these data, as well as secondary analysis of the latest census, household surveys, and existing research about the subsector, provided the basis for an analysis of needs, major initiatives, and recommendations for improvement.

The team working on the chapter on higher education conducted a survey of all universities in the country and in-depth interviews with the presidents of several of the large and some of the medium and small universities. Also, the team made observation visits to these institutions. Faculty, students, and employers were interviewed. This information and the review of existing research and documents about the sector provided the basis for the analysis of the subsector.

The team working in nonformal education organized several workshops with representatives from different types of NGOs working at this level. Using a participatory methodology, they negotiated the structure and content of the chapter. Using focus groups, the team working on management training interviewed employers, directors, and staff of the principal management training programs in the country. Also, they studied alternative models of organizing management training in other countries in the region and elsewhere.

The team working in the chapter of management and decentralization of education interviewed administrators in the Ministry of Education at all levels, mapped out how the different functions were carried out, and discussed how efficiency could be improved under various alternatives of decentralization. They examined the constraints posed by the legal framework and by the organizational structure of the ministry. A special emphasis of the chapter was on the improvement of the information system of the Ministry of Education. Also, there was emphasis in strengthening the functions of policy definition and in ways to improve the budget process.

During the preparation of the assessment there were numerous meetings among the teams preparing the different chapters which allowed an exchange of information and enrichment of each chapter with the perspectives and insights developed in other chapters. The final report included an introductory summary chapter of the main problems and overall recommendations of the assessment, examining their impact in quality, access, and efficiency. The summary explicitly developed connections between different chapters, for example, integrating the conclusions of the analysis of the economic scenario with those of the chapter of costs and financing and with those of the sectional chapters.

This assessment, which was completed in three months by more than thirty professionals working directly in the different teams, became the single most comprehensive document on education in El Salvador. It was published by a private university and, as discussed in Chapter 7, became a central point of reference for national dialogue in education.

The Importance of Contact with Policy Makers. An important feature that sector assessments share with evaluation of programs and with policy-oriented surveys is their emphasis on identification of the audience for the assessment. How this audience is defined and how it participates in the preparation of the assessment determines the difference the assessment makes in terms of shaping education policies.

Approaches to sector assessment differ in their emphasis on dissemination as opposed to dialogue. The IEES methodology, for example, recognizes the importance of defining a steering committee that will oversee the preparation of an assessment. IEES defines the host government as the main beneficiary of this activity and recommends that periodic briefings be provided to high-level policy makers and mid-level planners and administrators during the preparation of the assessment. Once the assessment is concluded, it is recommended that the sponsoring agency ensure widespread dissemination of the document as it can provide a common framework to others working in the education sector and facilitate external agency coordination (Pigozzi and Cieutat, 1988).

An alternative view gives more weight to the steering committee and to the role of the dialogue supported by the sector assessment. For instance, Kemmerer (1994) states the following three reasons for conducting a review and discussion of the findings, options, and recommendations at every stage of the preparation of a report:

1. Calculations and technical analysis only inform part of the effects of intended policy changes.
2. The analysis is usually limited to technical problems, but issues of implementation and political acceptability of the change ought to be considered in assessing policy changes.
3. In some cases, technical analysis does not lead directly to policy recommendations.

An important role of sector assessments is to stimulate national dialogue on education (Kemmerer, 1994). This involves dialogue between education and other sectors as well as dialogue within the sector. Sector assessments can serve to promote national discussions of education issues, expand the focus of education ministries to better take into account intersectional issues, promote collaboration between ministries, clarify goals for the sector, increase accountability, expand a support base for education reform, and build a forum for discussions of education (Kemmerer, 1994).

POLICY DIALOGUE AS NEGOTIATION

If the approach to inform education policy discussed in Chapter 4 sees policy dialogue as persuasion, the approach discussed in this chapter sees policy dialogue as negotiation. Common to both perspectives is the treatment of information as the product of rational inquiry and as independent and external to the user of information. In the first perspective, information leads directly to knowledge; it follows that technical analysis can lead directly to policy definition and decision making.

In the second perspective, we wish to distinguish between types of information. The process of knowledge utilization involves not just the information provided by the expert but that provided by the policy maker, such as goal preferences. The policy maker's information acts to filter the value of information supplied by the expert and labeled as rational or objective and to organize the policy maker's own decision processes.

The different methods, such as information systems, policy surveys, and sector assessments, can expand the knowledge of decision makers, but decision makers shape this knowledge by negotiating which topics are important and which bodies of data are more pertinent to inform certain issues. The decision maker is not, as in the approach of policy dialogue as persuasion, a passive recipient of precooked conclusions drawn from research but is an active agent with interests and with the power to select between alternative sources of information. Those interested in pursuing rational inquiry to inform policy must, therefore, engage their client from the outset. The problem of information use in this perspective cannot be an afterthought once the research or the analysis is completed. Research and analysis have to begin with the client in mind if they do not want to risk being irrelevant to the issues of concern to the policy maker. Deciding on an indicator to measure access to school requires negotiations about whether the best operational definition is one that measures enrollment in school at the beginning of the school year or some average of student attendance during the year. Designing a survey to understand why children repeat grades requires understanding why policy makers are interested in this problem and what are their frames of reference. Preparing a sector assessment starts with negotiations about the content and methods to carry out the assessment and continues with ongoing discussions as the assessment is prepared. In this perspective, researchers have to design research that is sensitive and that can speak to the questions the decision makers have and not to the questions researchers have, which may or may not interest policy makers.

However, even in this perspective there is a division between knowledge producers and knowledge consumers. Though there is a much higher appreciation for the client than in the perspective discussed in Chapter 4, and a higher appreciation for the importance of taking the client's needs and views into account at the outset of generating information, there is still a division of labor between the policy maker and the researcher and analyst. In this second perspective, there is a time for both of them to talk, and it is the client who decides how the knowledge produced by the researcher is used and contextualized. However, the task of generating knowledge is still seen as something that requires the independent work of highly-skilled professionals specialized in methods of social science research. Chapter 6 discusses a third perspective in which the lines that separate consumers from producers of research blur even further as policy makers and administrators become producers of the research they consume.

NOTES

1. See, for example, Network of Educational Innovation for Development in Africa, NEIDA; Educational Innovation Programme for Development in the Arab States, EIPDAS; Asia and Pacific Programme of Educational Innovation for Development, APEID; Caribbean Network of Educational Innovation for Development, CARNEID; and Cooperation for Reinforcing the Development of Education in Europe, CORDEE.

2. Basic Research and Implementation in Developing Education Systems (BRIDGES) was a seven-year USAID-funded initiative to generate knowledge about how to improve basic education in developing countries. The project was centered at Harvard University and involved collaboration from a number of institutions in the United States and abroad.

Chapter 6

Informing Policy by Constructing Knowledge

Chapters 4 and 5 trace a progression in the relationship between researchers and policy makers. They compare a perspective which sees the former as producers of knowledge and the latter as consumers of knowledge to a perspective which sees policy makers as critical actors in the research process. In this latter perspective, policy makers select which products of research to consume and help researchers frame the problems to be investigated so research can be most useful for policy.

In our opinion, there is a further step to be taken. In Chapter 5, policy analysts and experts are seen as mediators between the worlds of research and policy, but the two worlds are still considered as being separate. This chapter extends the relationship between research and policy. It proposes that researchers and policy makers live not separately but in the same world, and that through processes of reciprocal influence, they construct knowledge together. Two variations of this approach are discussed. In the first variation, we focus on the participation of senior policy makers in the research process. Then, we introduce a variation that goes back to our discussion of ministries of education as complex bureaucracies and proposes the participation of actors at multiple levels in the research process, within and outside the education bureaucracy.

These variations in participatory approaches to policy dialogue follow from the recognition that technical expertise does not give a person superior power to select among education goals. This is hard for experts and researchers to admit. Their extended training and constant mingling with people socialized in similar ways tends to make them unaware of the value choices which they make when analyzing policy options. Sometimes dialogue with others who do not share their training and who may not share their values uncovers these discrepancies about values. Naive technical experts explain away those discrepancies as a result of the lack of training of the policy maker. Of course, implicit in this explanation is another judgment which values certain forms of knowledge more than others.

Technical expertise is not always valued highly by decision makers and education administrators. Those who make decisions do not always recognize the special skills of those with high levels of training in research or technical knowledge. They tend to minimize the competence of experts to make choices about the fundamental goals of a society and, therefore, about the goals for the education system.

Decision makers are more responsive to highly influential political figures and to the political processes by which societies make fundamental choices than they are to researchers and technical analysts. From the perspective of the policy maker, one could question whether participation of researchers and technical experts in decision making makes any sense at all. Policy makers know that research does not solve value conflicts, they may not trust the wisdom of researchers, and they know that research results are fallible. However, it is interesting that most researchers, when they ponder over the merits of participation, tend to see this situation in reverse and presume to know what should be done.

We believe that, although policy formation is essentially a political and organizational process, it is possible to make better choices if effective ways can be found to merge this processes with technical analysis. We posit that the knowledge that can inform policy reform will be superior knowledge if it is not simply knowledge derived from the political process and if it is not simply the knowledge produced by researchers. Knowledge will be superior if appropriate ways are found by which knowledge can be constructed jointly by policy makers and researchers.

The two variations of this view stem from two different ways to answer the question of who makes policy. In the first variation, policy is made by senior officials at the top of the education bureaucracy. In the second variation, policy is formed by all actors in the organization and by those whose interests are affected by the organization, namely, external stakeholders. This second perspective treats participation as an end in itself. If we assume that collective choices should reflect the value preferences of those affected, democratic participation of those affected by the choices is necessary to celebrate value preferences.

In addition to being an end in itself, participation is also a means to having better policies. Participation creates ownership in policy reform proposals which will facilitate implementation. The importance of participation and ownership for the successful implementation of education policies is beginning to receive some attention. At a recent meeting of African ministers and permanent secretaries of education, participation was discussed in the context of ownership of plans. A background paper prepared for the meeting listed the many factors hindering the successful implementation of activities to improve and expand education in sub-Saharan Africa. National conditions, and how they influence effective implementation, were analyzed and the ownership of the various programs discussed.

Mauritius provided an excellent example of how a national education plan could actually be formulated and implemented using local expertise . . . with the help of many partners (professionals, political leaders, the private sector, etc.). It is a complex process involving a lot of learning-by-doing, negotiation, and the progressive development of national capacity. [This emphasizes] the need for programs to be based on clear objectives defined by consulting all the partners involved. This helps to encourage participation and create a sense of ownership among all stakeholders. (Donors to African Education Task Force, 1993)

Participation also improves the quality of the knowledge generated to inform options because it brings the experience and perspectives of people who are directly affected by the consequences of those choices to bear on the examination of alternatives.

A review of developing country experience with planning concluded that the limitations on the information available to planners who rely only on analytic techniques result in less-than-optimal solutions. This review concluded that qualitative judgment is an essential ingredient in policy analysis, and that such judgment is best informed by consultation "not only in different parts of the government, but also with businessmen and academics. Japan, Korea, and Brazil have, for some time, employed consultation to improve their economic management" (Agarwala, 1983, 16).

This is consistent with the view that solving complex problems is a process of finding successive approximations, that any given answer to the problem can always be improved, and that only open dialogue allows people to deal productively with such problems (Senge, 1990).

There are many drawbacks to a participatory approach to creating knowledge to support policy change. The first one is that participation takes time. This does not necessarily mean that participation is costly. While it is true that participatory processes will increase costs in the analysis and design stage of the policy, if we think of policy formation as extending into implementation, participation may substantially decrease costs at the latter stage, making up for the increased up-front costs.

Another difficulty is that educational researchers and planners are not well trained in participatory methodologies. Some may see participation as an implicit recognition of the limitations of their expertise, which they value so highly.

Planners avoid formal participatory schemes for several of the following reasons:

- Participatory schemes are time and resource consuming. The complex task of resolving the multiple interests of a large set of stakeholders cannot easily be accomplished in an open democratic forum.
- Participatory schemes are too demanding on participants. Clients and beneficiaries are not necessarily sufficiently involved and capable of resolving issues.
- Participatory schemes require complete openness and disclosure. As we shall see, this is not always desirable or possible.
- Planners are not trained in participatory management. They do not want to relinquish what little authority they happen to have and fear that their professional autonomy will be challenged (Benveniste, 1991, 47).

A major difficulty with participatory approaches in education policy dialogue is that many organizational and political cultures are not supportive of participation and democracy. Public administration in some countries is highly hierarchical and participatory approaches represent a major cultural change. That does not mean that cultures cannot change, but change takes time and requires a strategy to counteract the sources of resistance likely to emerge. Because of this variation in country contexts there is no standard approach to using participation. Negotiating a shared vision in different contexts requires craft and political savvy, ability to identify windows of opportunity, capacity to build coalitions in support of the approach, and ability to stay the course in the face of opposition.

PARTICIPATION OF POLICY MAKERS
IN THE RESEARCH PROCESS

The dialogue between researchers or analysts and policy makers proposed in the last three variations of the approach discussed in Chapter 5 (i.e., information systems, policy surveys, and sector assessments) was proposed as a way to help researchers understand the frames of reference of those who make decisions. This dialogue also informs policy makers of the frames of reference and the methods employed by researchers to construct knowledge. There are three possible stages in this process of dialogue. At an early stage, policy makers and researchers collaborate in the design of research. At a second stage, the dialogue is extended to the analysis of the data and to drawing inferences to give meaning to these data. Finally, researchers and policy makers can collaborate by going beyond the data into designing and implementing policy reform.

Design of the Research

Collaboration in research design is a logical extension of the dialogue already proposed. When this dialogue between researcher and policy maker takes place at the outset, it is difficult to distinguish whether the policy maker is simply informing the researcher of his or her own frames of reference or whether the policy maker is actually contributing to the design of the research. The survey we discussed which assesses the implementation of a bilingual education project in Paraguay illustrates the difficulty of distinguishing the direction of influence.

In 1996, the director of the curriculum unit who was in charge of implementing a pilot project to teach Guarani-speaking children in their mother tongue in Paraguay invited the HIID resident advisor to a meeting. The project had sponsored a number of surveys and studies in other areas and there was a solid relationship of trust between the director of curriculum and the resident advisor of the Harvard project. Bilingual education at that time was an exceedingly sensitive subject in Paraguay. The pilot program was controversial. Many people inside and outside the ministry claimed that parents were outraged at the fact that their children would not learn Spanish in school, that teachers opposed the program, and that there were problems with the implementation of the program. The director of curriculum explained to the Harvard advisor that she was puzzled because her personal knowledge, based on visits she had made to some schools participating in the program and on reports she received from her staff, suggested that things were going well. She acknowledged that it would be possible that her staff, committed to the program, would be presenting a biased view to her, but she also thought it was possible that the arguments advanced by those who saw problems with the project were a reflection of their personal biases rather than a mere translation of facts. She proposed a survey to obtain the views from teachers participating in the program. She wanted to ask about the difficulties with implementation and about the teachers' perceptions of how parents and students responded to the program.

There were several meetings to prepare the questionnaire. In those meetings the director of curriculum and the senior staff in charge of the program of bilingual education explained the areas in which they were interested. The advisor contributed his expertise in questionnaire design and survey administration. The director of curriculum and her associates quickly understood the logic of good survey questions and the biases which could result from the survey and from its administration. As a consequence, they ended up designing most of the questions themselves. At the same time, the advisor learned about which issues of the bilingual education program were of most concern to them and the main questions regarding the implementation of the program. As he learned more about the nuances of bilingual education in Paraguay, he suggested questions of policy relevance. The advisor was persuaded by the director of curriculum and her colleagues of the importance of obtaining information not just about facts and the behaviors and practices of teachers but about their attitudes and opinions about the program. Realizing that time was of the essence to the policy makers, he yielded in his initial stance that it would not be possible to obtain information about learning gains without proper measures of student achievement and suggested several ways to ask teachers about their perceptions of students' learning gains.

In this process of dialogue, the policy makers changed the researcher. He was certain that because he had made so many methodological compromises he could never hope to use the results for an academic publication. He would be very cautious when sharing the survey and the results with his colleagues at his academic home. At the same time, the researcher influenced the questions the policy makers asked about the program and the way they formulated them and collected them. The final questionnaire was very much a joint effort where the independent contribution of each specialist could not be distinguished. The questionnaire evolved over several series of discussions and revisions of drafts in the office of the director of curriculum. In the end, the director and her staff felt that the survey was very much their survey, and the researcher felt that the survey was his own.

Analysis of Data

The collaboration between researcher and policy maker can extend into the analysis of the data. Most data analysis is conducted in iterative stages where the results of early rounds of analysis inform successive rounds. Policy surveys in which data are collected to inform a predetermined model and where the analysis plan is fully elaborated before the data are collected are rare; we have never seen one in our work. Most researchers analyzing policy surveys go on fishing expeditions once the data are collected even if they had a preliminary model of hypotheses at the time of survey design. Taking the policy maker along on the expedition is good not only to increase the acceptance of the results of the analysis but to guide a better analysis process. Preliminary results can spark questions which only policy makers, with their experience and from their perspective facing education problems, can formulate. While researchers are trained to guide much of their analysis on the basis of the statistical significance of the differences they find when comparing groups, policy makers are more sensitive to the practical significance of the findings. These different sensitivities can lead to different routes in pursuing a line of analysis.

In our experience, however, training policy makers to grasp the fundamentals of research design and methodology is easier than training them in the fundamentals of hypothesis testing and statistical analysis. The dialogue at the analysis stage has generally been mediated by sessions to translate the results of the analysis, or the statistical differences observed, into simple conclusions in plain language. Once that translation is made decision makers can then suggest further lines of questioning to inform the analysis. This has been easier to do for simpler forms of analysis, such as analysis of descriptive statistics or basic measures of association between variables. Dialogue at the analysis stage using multivariate or multilevel analysis methodologies has only been possible in those rare cases where policy makers have had advanced statistical training. However, one can advance a long way in the understanding of a policy problem relying on descriptive statistics and the analysis of basic associations when the policy maker is on board and fully comprehends what is going on.

If, in the end, all knowledge is personal knowledge, one should ponder whether it is reasonable to expect that policy makers will be able to assimilate results of research when they cannot understand the methods used to draw the conclusions. It is quite possible that policy makers always need a personal reference to internalize the results of research and to make it personal knowledge. If that is the case, the results obtained with methods that are beyond their personal understanding will only be accepted when they confirm their views; that is, when there are other personal references that validate these findings. To expect that policy makers would be willing to disconfirm their personal knowledge on the basis of knowledge generated using procedures they do not comprehend would be to assume that they have a greater faith in the scientific method than in the other sources which inform their personal knowledge.

Paraguay. In the analysis of the data of the survey about the implementation of the bilingual education project, dialogue sessions continued between the director of curriculum, her staff, and the advisor. They looked together at reams of output as it came out of the computer. At several times, questions which were raised in these conversations led to immediate analysis of relationships. All those present looked over the shoulder of the advisor and directly at the computer screen. After scanning hundreds of cross-tabulations and differences between means, it was not clear that the director of curriculum or her staff could explain the meaning of a *p* value or of an *F* value in an analysis of variance, but they knew how to read the distribution of cases in rows and columns in a cross-tabulation and could explain what a significant *chi-square* or *anova* meant given those distributions. In this analysis, we did a great many cross-tabulations and contrasts which were not of obvious value to the advisor but which made eminent sense once the policy makers used the results to formulate an explanation of what was happening. These policy makers were more than informed consumers of analyses that could be carried out by someone else. They knew what they were looking for better than the analyst did and they knew how to make meaning out of the data in ways which escaped the competencies of the advisor.

El Salvador. Another example of participation of policy makers in the analysis of data is based in our experience in the education sector assessment in El Salvador. Several drafts of the various chapters were distributed among critical audiences for the assessment. The teams in charge of each chapter received guidance indicating the importance of circulating drafts, providing time for audiences to read them, and setting times to receive feedback and to take it seriously. This was done for several reasons. The basic reason is that our experience taught us that people were more likely to read drafts than to read final versions of a document. A draft for comments has a more definite deadline and a greater sense of urgency than does a final report. There is an immediate reason to read it. Also, we had learned that it was important to make sure reports were written in a way which could be understood by their intended audience. The only way to be sure was to discuss some version of the report with them. Although ongoing dialogue between researchers and policy makers helped the former understand better the type of evidence and language which would communicate more to their audience, the final test was to distribute some drafts and see how they were understood. A third reason for wide dissemination of drafts was to improve the quality of the analysis of the data. For several of the chapters, the readers challenged the inferences which had been drawn from the data and how the evidence was being read. Their observations were taken into account by the researchers in the final write up. For example, the chapter on basic education was perceived by the ministry as giving too little weight to two major initiatives of the ministry to improve access and quality. It became obvious in the discussion of the early drafts that the ministry had many detailed questions about these programs—questions it would be unwise to ignore. Further analysis was carried out and the appropriate sections expanded in the final version of the report.

In other cases this dialogue made it possible to identify different ways of reading the evidence. For instance, the evidence which showed limited differences between the EDUCO schools and ordinary rural schools (discussed in Chapter 1) was interpreted by the ministry in a way which explained that the sample was weighted in favor of schools where EDUCO had expanded one grade, rather than new schools which had been established under the program. The data collected could not settle differences in interpretation about the meaning of the evidence, but the different perspectives could be acknowledged in the final report, making it more balanced.

The dialogue between researchers and policy makers in the El Salvador sector assessment generated a number of conflicts. At times, researchers felt their professional autonomy and competency were being challenged by policy makers. At other times, policy makers felt their authority and performance were being questioned by the researchers. Most of these conflicts were resolved when both groups looked together at the evidence and discussed ways to interpret it and how to obtain additional evidence to contextualize the findings. The end result was that the researchers were changed by this process, becoming more sensitive to the perspective of policy makers. Policy makers also changed their perspectives, sharing with researchers a factual basis for the discussions. The process of analyzing the evidence benefited from this conflict and the dialogue that ensued.

Design and Implementation of Policies

The approach discussed in Chapter 5 proposes that, contrary to the view of policy dialogue as persuasion, policy design and implementation are the domain of the policy maker and not of the researcher or analyst. The approach we describe in this chapter comes full circle. It proposes that once the researcher has opened up to listen to and understand the policy maker, and once both have worked together designing and analyzing the results of research, the researcher can be invited to go beyond the realm of the analysis of the data. He or she can join the policy maker in drawing inferences and inventing what should be done to improve the problem both were trying to understand in the first place.

The dialogue between researchers and policy makers moves naturally to this third stage, flowing from the dialogue which designs the research and analyzes the results. Collaboration in the design stage flowed from the stage in which researchers listen to and try to understand the perspectives of policy makers. At this point, as both groups collaborate to make meaning out of the data, the dialogue flows beyond the data into what should be done to change and improve the reality that they have been trying to understand together.

This evolution is possible because of the interaction which is established in earlier stages and because of the trust that develops between research and policy maker. To many policy makers, trust is a more important base for legitimacy than expertise. Only if collaboration in earlier stages has developed into mutual trust will collaboration reach this stage of policy design. Just as researchers are traditionally defensive of their territory of research design and conclusion drawing, policy makers are traditionally defensive of their territory of policy making. But collaboration in earlier stages, and the processes of reciprocal influence between researcher and policy maker, can give researchers, in the eyes of policy makers, the credibility to participate in the formulation of policies. Collaboration at earlier stages of design and analysis forms the basis of trust which enables researchers to be invited to the domains of policy design and implementation. The extended collaboration between researcher and policy maker provides a basis on which to judge competencies and intentions of advisors and permits the establishment of relations of trust and mutual respect necessary for collaboration in the more sensitive domain of formulating policy.

In El Salvador, the coordinator of the sector assessment had weekly meetings with the minister of education and her closest advisors to discuss the progress of the assessment. Different members of the research groups would participate in these meetings. Over time, the minister gave more leeway to the coordinator in terms of making policy recommendations. This was possible not only because of the personal relationship of trust and respect which was established but because the coordinator came to understand and appreciate the perspective of the minister. In preparation for these meetings, he could anticipate many questions or concerns which would be expressed by the minister at the meeting and communicate them to the members of the research team. The advisor was asked to make recommendations in the assessment, to give suggestions for the design of programs of the ministry, and to give feedback about ongoing activities of the ministry.

In Paraguay, the resident advisor of the technical assistance project also had weekly meetings with the minister of education and with senior policy makers to discuss the results of a sector assessment as they evolved. A relationship of trust and respect developed between policy makers and the researcher to the point that the opinions of the advisor were sought to validate the legitimacy of the advice offered by other short-term consultants from the same advisory team. There were many times when the advisor was asked to comment on proposed education legislation and to make suggestions for major new and ongoing programmatic initiatives. When requests for advice reached the domains of possible changes among senior ministry staff, it became clear that there was more trust than was justified by the competencies of the advisor. It was also apparent to the advisor that some of the fundamental questions of interest to policy makers, such as up to what grade to continue with education in children's mother tongue, could not be answered from research.

As the dialogue between researchers and policy makers continues, the boundary between these two activities softens. Each changes the other, and together they construct knowledge which can inform policy. Here, policy is understood as that initiated by senior officials at the top of the education organization. Now we discuss an alternative meaning of policy dialogue as we expand our definition of who makes policy.

POLICY DIALOGUE AS ORGANIZATIONAL LEARNING

Chapter 2 proposed two alternative meanings for policy, namely, one that defines policy as the objectives and plans of organizations and one that defines policies as transactions where intentions and implementation blend into a seamless management process. Chapter 3 developed further the notion of why education policies are so difficult to inform and characterized the complexity of education systems in terms of their internal structure and of their external environment. This chapter takes account of this proposed complexity characterizing policy dialogue as organizational learning.

Who Are the Actors in the Policy Making Process?

Our discussion of various approaches to inform policy for education focuses on policy as decided by senior administrators placed at the top of the education bureaucracy. This is consistent with most literature on research and knowledge utilization which assumes that the analyst is in the role of advising a single decision maker who is highly placed in the organizational hierarchy and has authority to decide on directions for education policy reform. Who in fact makes policy? Education reforms are more than the intentions of senior leaders sitting in the top of the bureaucracy, and they are more than regulations and norms. Live education reforms are made by mid-level administrators, by principals, by teachers, and by parents; their understandings, attitudes, and competencies are the foundation of meaningful change in the classroom. If research is to inform change, it has to help these stakeholders of the education process change their understandings, their attitudes, their skills, and motivations. Change will come about not just because high-level administrators can pull some policy levers that will trigger change in an education machinery, but because a number of people will understand and want to do things differently.

Our search for the actors that matter begins in the classroom and at the school. The actors include the parents and students who decide to participate in school and to support school work at home. They include teachers and principals and the larger communities where schools are located. They include supervisors and local authorities and politicians. They include administrators in the Ministry of Education, who distribute materials and information, make appointments and transfers, and who can channel requests from teachers and communities. They include high-level officials in the ministry, those responsible for teacher training, for curriculum design, and for evaluation and administration, and those in charge of budgeting and disbursement. Stakeholders also include ministers of education and their peers in the cabinet and social leaders who can exert influence in the education system or in politicians.

The interaction between these levels is systemic and synergistic. What each level does is reinforced or resisted by the levels above and below. Each of these levels of stakeholders represents a system which is interlocked with the other systems. Each defines the degrees of freedom of the other and has their degrees of freedom defined by the rest.

Change should proceed at all levels at the same time. The hope of initiating change at a single point in the system, be it the center of the education bureaucracy or the school, makes sense only if it radiates to other levels.

When Research Helps Organizations Learn

If every manager in the education system is a policy maker, and if dialogue between researchers and policy makers leads to reciprocal influence of one group on the other, it is possible for the boundaries between research and management to fade even further. As participation in policy formation opens up to education administrators and teachers at different levels of the system and to the stakeholders for change external to the education bureaucracy, research should adopt a different function in order to inform these public conversations.

From this perspective, the function of research is absorbed by managers as they apply their methods to the construction of knowledge in order to obtain a better understanding of the problems they are trying to solve and of the options available to do this. The products of research and analysis become part of a collective public conversation and part of the shared sets of meanings of all stakeholders who act within the education system. Managers adopt the approach of the experimental scientist and use research to assess the impact of new initiatives. Risk taking is encouraged in an organizational culture that values change. Research methods are ways to assess the results of the risks taken.

This view conceives of lasting educational change as the result of organizational learning of the different interlocking components of the education system. Dialogue is necessary for this learning to occur. Organizations cannot learn from their experience if people who work in them have no information about the results of their actions, clarity about their purposes, or the possibility to explore alternatives to achieve these shared objectives. Dialogue is a necessary condition to build that shared vision about objectives, to assess experience, and to explore alternatives.

When we say dialogue, we mean more than casual conversations among colleagues. We understand dialogue to be a disciplined participation in an exploration of strengths and weaknesses of a collective project. Research is a powerful tool to provide information which can support this dialogue. Planning about the future is an almost natural consequence of this dialogue.

Education reforms become alive when in every school, teachers, students, and parents begin a systematic reflection about the conditions which influence their own learning and begin to organize actions to improve those conditions. The emphasis here is on groups rather than individuals as the target for organizational change. The assumption is that it takes several persons, together, to accept and support each other in a change effort.

This type of dialogue and participation may run counter to tradition and culture in society at large, in the public sector, or in the Ministry of Education. Therefore, fostering it requires staying the course even in the face of adversity. An additional problem is that in societies where civil society is weak, opening up participation for policy formation at the local level may be tantamount to empowering local party bosses who will control the openings and how they are used. Assuming this risk and monitoring the possible unintended effects is necessary as a long-term strategy to achieve sustainable change.

To make this kind of organizational learning possible, the following five conditions are necessary:

1. Lack of fear
2. Opportunities to reflect
3. Opportunities to dialogue
4. Opportunities to practice
5. Opportunities to assess practice and reflect and dialogue

These conditions allow change at the individual level in terms of developing new cognitions and behaviors among ministry staff and other stakeholders, but they go beyond the individual into facilitating change in groups, therefore changing the situational factors that shape the way individuals behave. Dialogue as a strategy to change individuals is particularly important in ministries of education because it permits exchanging information, developing skills, and influencing attitudes and cognitions. Given that ministries have constraints on two other major approaches to influence individual change in organizations, namely staff selection and removal, this emphasis is well founded. As a mechanism to permit information exchange, dialogue makes it possible to reach agreement on what changes are wanted and the rationale for the changes. Dialogue can do more than promote information exchange; it can go deeper by helping individuals accept change, especially if it is structured in a series of iterations that permit reflection, dialogue, practice, and assessment over and over again. This will promote cognitive and attitudinal change and will help develop new skills.

In addition to these changes at the individual level promoted by the proposed cycle of reflection, dialogue, practice, and assessment, dialogue can increase learning and heighten commitment to the change agenda as dialogue takes place in groups. In many ministries of education there are very limited opportunities for communication across different units. Consequently, it is not uncommon to find incoherence and contradictions between initiatives undertaken by the ministry. Also, it is common that few change efforts take the time to identify the relevant stakeholders and to communicate clearly what is expected of each of them to support the change. There is no shared vision guiding education actions. Opportunities for dialogue at all levels within the ministry and education organizations and between the ministry and other stakeholders of change are essential to gain a minimum sense of common direction.

Because the tenure of many senior administrators in their office is too short, the permanent staff of the ministry become skeptical about change and the sustainability of change. Dialogue within units is necessary to energize and mobilize the permanent staff in support of change efforts. It takes leadership and charisma to initiate and sustain this process of dialogue. In our experience people working in ministries of education are looking for ways to find meaning in what they do so they can respond favorably to initiatives to engage them in worthwhile efforts. Persistent leadership will be necessary to convince them that this will not be yet another failed or short-lived attempt to change.

An example of policy dialogue as organizational learning is the project of technical assistance of HIID to the Ministry of Education in Paraguay. This case is discussed in detail in Chapter 7. The purpose of the project, which started in mid-1995, was to strengthen the capacity of the ministry to carry out research and planning. The first activity was to support the preparation of a strategic education plan. To carry out the plan, a strategic dialogue group was formed, including all senior managers of the Ministry of Education and the members of a National Advisory Committee to the Education Reform. A small policy analysis unit was formed to coordinate the preparation of technical reports which would inform the discussions of the dialogue group. The objective of this activity was to achieve a shared set of understandings among senior ministry officials of the main problems of education, of a set of options, and of a strategy to overcome them. This proposed strategy would then be discussed with a greater set of stakeholders inside and outside the Ministry of Education.

The strategic dialogue group agreed on the objectives of the activity and defined the procedural rules to guide the discussions which would take place every week for two hours. An outline for the analysis of the education sector was agreed upon. The policy analysis unit began to coordinate the organization of task forces to prepare the reports, later discussed in the dialogue group. The format of each report was simple. It identified the major issues in the subsector, examined ongoing activities, and discussed possible reform activities currently not under consideration. The policy analysis unit coordinated assistance from national and international consultants to work with the task forces. Each task force included members of the policy analysis unit, the senior manager in charge of the subsector discussed, several managers of that unit, one or more members of the advisory council to the reform, and the consultants. The preparation of each paper took approximately two weeks. The papers were concise and to the point, not to exceed twenty pages, and were distributed to all members of the strategic dialogue group a few days prior to the meeting.

The initial discussions of the strategic dialogue group were facilitated by a specialist in group dynamics and organizational communication who provided feedback at the end of each session as to whether the group was adhering to the agreed upon rules.

The discussions of the group were stimulated by the reports coordinated by the policy analysis unit and by a series of applied studies conducted by an education research unit. The weekly meetings of the group alternated between discussions of these reports and a management training seminar designed to develop skills in communication, strategic planning, budgeting, programming, staff supervision, leadership, implementation, use of basic management software, and similar topics.

After several weeks of this routine, the group had achieved greater cohesion than when the project started. Senior managers of the ministry communicated better with one another, they used research-based information to focus discussions about the implementation of the reform and about further options for change, and they had developed greater confidence in their own professional skills and understanding of the problems confronting the sector. They had opened up to criticism and could focus on discussing issues without confronting each other in the meetings. At the end of five months, the strategic dialogue group had discussed about 2,000 pages of research reports and reviews of the major topics of the education system, including primary, secondary, technical, tertiary, financing, management, decentralization, special, bilingual, and adult education. They had completed a sector assessment. This was summarized in a document, called *The Education Challenge. A Proposal for Dialogue*, which would be discussed with a large group of stakeholders for education change. In preparation for these larger discussions, the strategic dialogue group completed the cycle of training with an intensive workshop on strategic negotiation and conflict resolution.

The proposal for dialogue was then presented and discussed at more than twenty roundtables attended by an average of thirty persons each, covering different ministries (i.e., finance, planning, and health), all education supervisors and teacher union leaders, state governors and mayors, political leaders, members of congress, representatives of nongovernment organizations, university presidents and administrators, church and social leaders, representatives of private schools, business leaders, and other groups. The proposal was also discussed by each director of the ministry of education with their senior- and mid-level staff. These roundtables were workshops which lasted four to sixteen hours, depending on time availability of the group consulted. Participants received the document in advance, listened to a summary presentation, and participated in a discussion of some or all of the topics covered in the proposal for dialogue while making recommendations. The moderators of the discussion were members of the strategic dialogue group who participated actively in the exchange, ensuring that the discussion was informed by the results of the 2,000 pages of analysis which had been examined during the initial five months of the project. Each participant in a roundtable was invited to organize further sessions of discussion if they so desired and to provide written feedback and recommendations to the strategic dialogue group by a specified date.

The discussions in which the strategic dialogue group engaged, as well as those which involved other stakeholders, served primarily to construct collectively knowledge about the problems of the education system. Each participant in the discussions brought their own experience to this collective learning in order to interpret the results of analysis and research.

This dialogue among national level stakeholders on education reform was accompanied by dialogue at the school level. The reform encouraged the establishment of circles of learning at the school level, including teachers and principals, who would discuss the fundamental goals of the reform and their specific problems and needs, and who would develop a local plan of change. To facilitate these discussions at the school level, the research unit conducted seven case studies of effective schools and produced a book which described those schools and explained why they were effective. The format of the book emphasized study-and-discussion questions and proposed a series of questions to characterize the dynamics of each school in terms of management, classroom practices, and links with the community. This book was distributed to every teacher, principal, and supervisor in the country.

PART III

Case Studies of
Use of Information in
Policy Making

The six chapters in this part are case studies of deliberate attempts to inform education policy with research and policy analysis activities in developing countries. Each of the cases is based on documented experience. We discuss how the different approaches to informing policy are illustrated by the cases. However, the cases lack the precise boundaries which distinguish one approach from another. Aspects of various approaches are found in the same case. Also, the cases are a sample of convenience and were selected from examples about which we had first-hand, in-depth knowledge because we thought they would help to illustrate some of the issues that we discuss. The cases are not intended to be exemplary in any other way. There are several biases in this selection associated with the fact that all the cases reflect examples in which there were opportunities for collaboration between national counterparts and foreign advisors. For obvious reasons, our work as foreign advisors made us more knowledgeable of those types of cases. The cases could have been chosen on a different basis other than relying so intensely on personal experience. We opted to be consistent with our own belief that all knowledge is personal. With the exception of the Namibia case, we drew primarily on personal sources of knowledge. We trust readers will be critical and will be able, in light of their own experience and in light of the limitations of our own experience, to construct their own personal knowledge and deconstruct our conclusions.

Chapter 7

The Etosha Conference
in Namibia

This case describes how broad public discussions about education issues can generate information useful to policy makers. Research methods are used to identify issues that will focus public attention and structure a discussion process. In 1988, Namibia was two years into the implementation of a national education policy to expand basic education to nine years and, consequently, reform the curriculum and make it more responsive to the needs of the economy.

The implementation of this reform was being assisted by a long-term project funded by USAID. It became clear to those responsible for the reform that feedback was needed to improve implementation. A consultant from IEES organized a national conference to obtain this type of feedback. The conference served both as a mechanism to disseminate existing knowledge about critical problem areas of the reform and to obtain feedback on possible avenues to address these problems.

The first consultation took place in April 1988. The conference was structured to address the following three major themes:

1. Communication and consultation mechanisms to open up the ministry to feedback from local schools and communities
2. Links between education, training, and employment, and the role of education in employment and training
3. Curriculum adequacy and relevance for the Namibian context

These issues were selected because prior studies indicated that they were critical areas in the implementation of the reform. For example, the need for better communication channels had been established in the following earlier evaluation report produced by an evaluation task force of the Secondary Education Improvement project: "Many teachers and parents want to understand the educational programme better. The expansion has come so quickly that many people need further information and support for effective implementation" (Snyder, 1991).

The conference lasted four days. Participants represented a wide spectrum of stakeholders in education reform from the capital city area. They included parents, teachers, principals, education officers, employers in the private sector, politicians, university faculty, and central and district public education officers. A total of 116 persons participated in the conference and attendance was very high at each session.

The conference organized participants into smaller groups (fifteen groups of eight persons each) to discuss each of the themes. Each theme was introduced with a videotape. The video presented interviews to parents and teachers from an array of communities. The objective of the videos was to provoke discussion bringing in feedback, sometimes critical, about the Nine-Year Basic Education program. The videotaped interviews were chosen to provide this feedback, rather than statistical information, because organizers believed that they would communicate better to the audience of the conference. The scripts of the videos were prepared on the basis of existing knowledge about the problems confronting the reform; they were visual presentations of a report for discussion. The following excerpt from the video on communication illustrates the content of the tapes:

[Off-camera voice]: It appears that many people see the government as having taken over the community schools, a belief that has been strengthened by a serious misunderstanding that has arisen over the selection of children to attend secondary schools.

[School principal interviewed]: Well, the reluctance of the community to participate in these schools came because of the mishandling of the government in the whole thing, in that I think they were not informed at first on how the selection of the first grade was going to be handled. I think if they had tried to inform the public they wouldn't have been so offended. Now I feel that since everything was mishandled so that way they feel that they have to take it back and see what the government is going to do about the whole situation.

[Junior secondary teacher]: We as teachers have really got no idea what the government policy is, or what they are trying to do, because we don't know what they are going to do with the Cs and Ds, whether they will find a school for them.

Videos were then followed by panel discussions, participants in the panels were people who had access to state-of-the-art knowledge on the issues discussed, many of them came from university-based research centers or faculty. The panels were a mechanism to provide research-based information on the subjects discussed. Some of this research was also disseminated in summaries of studies (particularly on the subject of training and employment) included in the packets distributed to the participants.

After the panel presentations, small groups participated in discussions of the issues raised and made recommendations. The results of the small group discussions were then presented in a plenary session. The focus of the small group discussions was to identify specific recommendations. In her opening speech, the Permanent Secretary of Education defined the task ahead of the small groups as follows:

We hope you will now work with your colleagues on the tasks set for your group, rather than engaging in endless debates about the "ultimate" purpose of education. We shall be looking for answers to who, what, and how. For example, in communication, who is it that needs to be informed and who needs to do the informing, what information is needed, and how do we improve information flow and two-way communication. (Permanent Secretary of Education, cited in Snyder, 1991)

The conference was highly successful in that it provided a mechanism to bring formative feedback to those responsible for the implementation of the reform. "Although it would be difficult to capture the full emotional and intellectual involvement of everyone at this conference, it had the atmosphere of an important event" (Snyder, 1991).

Participants gave the conference high ratings in a final evaluation, as summarized in the following report of the organizing committee:

Comments were very complimentary (e.g. "The arrangements and structure could not have been better," "Group work utilization was excellent," "This conference is a long overdue exercise . . . it is forums of this nature that accord further innovations," "Many a conference should run along these lines for effectiveness; it was structured in a way that made participants feel at ease—people were very actively involved—very well run—very professional," "Been a useful conference," "There were quite a variety of activities keeping the participants busy hence the good attendance on all the conference days," "Production of materials was good," "Structure well representative of cross-section of interests—so very well structured," "Very worthwhile," "We need this kind of conference country wide.") One person called the conference the "Great Education Debate." (Snyder, 1991)

This initial conference was followed by two other conferences in other parts of the country. A major outcome of these three conferences is that it led to further calls for the formation of a New National Education Commission to review the objectives and programs of the reform. Also, it institutionalized a series of community meetings, building on the tradition of community meetings to explain at the local level the objectives of the reform. The traditional community meetings inspired the format of the conference, as seen in the following:

One of the strengths of our systems has been the Community meeting— roughly translated as community consultation. We talk through our problems and concerns. Even when solutions are not immediate, the consultation increases our understanding and unity. This is our broad goal for this conference—to come together, to present our different perspectives on the issues in the educational system, and to formulate the general outline of targets, strategies and structures to address these issues. (Permanent Secretary of Education, cited in Snyder, 1991)

At some point in this follow-up process, the minister of education became very defensive about the feedback he was receiving, but the other ministry personnel recognized the importance of what they heard. The initial USAID reaction was concern because so much discussion and agitation had been created. Eventually, the value of the conference was widely appreciated. The minister was subsequently replaced.

The consultative meetings also worked as mechanisms to provide ongoing feedback about implementation activities. "Unfortunately, again, the process was viewed as successful but very risky. It hasn't been continued systematically by subsequent ministry regimes. It did help the curriculum work in concrete terms and so had some technical payoff" (Snyder, 1994).

The Etosha Conference in Namibia illustrates elements of the approaches discussed in Chapters 4 and 5. The identification of stakeholders and preparation of videos and conference packets to disseminate the results of research on important themes is a way to influence the formation of a policy agenda using research-based knowledge as ammunition. The solicitation of feedback from participants on key aspects of the implementation of the reform represents a similar consultation procedure to the one discussed in Chapter 5.

The defensive reaction of the minister of education and the perception that successive ministers had of the consultative meetings as risky illustrates how public discussion of policy can be resisted by senior decision makers accustomed to more authoritarian styles.

The invitation of the Permanent Secretary to discuss what to do as opposed to discussing education goals is significant given our contention that policy formation by necessity relates to goals and values. It is possible that dialogue is easier when goals and values are not discussed directly but indirectly through the specific actions that they suggest.

Chapter 8

Conducting an Education Sector Assessment in Egypt

This case illustrates the importance of the relationship between research and policy making as a determinant of use of research products. Some policy makers look for research to justify policies that have already been decided. Researchers unable to communicate in the national language are limited in their ability to understand the culture in which they are working. Relationships of trust with national officials take longer to develop.

BACKGROUND

Although a fair amount had been written about education in Egypt prior to 1989, empirical assessments were limited to programs and subsectors. Visiting representatives from international and bilateral assistance agencies had reviewed separately primary, technical, secondary, and higher education. Their reports provided some empirical data about specific programs but did not show linkages or problems between levels (e.g., between primary and secondary) or discuss the performance of the system in meeting national objectives.

The only published assessment of the education system as a system in Egypt provided little empirical evidence to support its assertions about the quality and operation of schools.

Contacts with Egyptian colleagues suggested that a number of empirical studies on education were to be found in Egyptian universities in the form of master's and doctoral dissertations written in Arabic. Several efforts were made to generate a bibliography and to do a review of this research, but ministry officials demonstrated little interest in the review and the project was abandoned.

Statistical data about the education system were limited to annual yearbooks that carried data aggregated at the district and state levels. The statistics were published in the second year after their collection and were not used in the annual planning and budgeting cycles. Instead, information for annual plans and budgets was obtained by each department (primary, textbooks, curriculum, teacher training, secondary, and technical education) using their own administrative staff. These data were not collated or kept from year to year and were not used for evaluation of the Ministry of Education. Statistical data from universities were limited to enrollments by programs. There were a number of institutional studies, some in the form of dissertations, but these had not been collated nor had any systemwide evaluation based on statistics been carried out.

Of course, there were evaluations of the education system. In Egypt, as elsewhere, education is a major determinant of the life chances of individuals and is often in the public eye. Newspapers carried comments regularly, mostly critical, comparing the declining quality of the education system to previous golden years. Most of these criticisms were limited to single policies or to single programs. Critiques of the system focused on single factors, such as lack of commitment by teachers or lack of parental support, but there were no analyses available that indicated how things had come to be the way they were and how to overcome them. There was no large vision of what an education system should be, nor any plan of how to get there.

THE IMPETUS TO REFORM

The turning point was the appointment in December 1986 of a new minister of education. The new minister was distinguished by several unique attributes. He had for several years served as Egypt's representative to the United Nations Educational, Scientific, and Cultural Organization (UNESCO), where he had read widely in research and theory about education and development. His appointment as minister coincided with the second term of a powerful president, who shared his belief that education was Egypt's key to economic growth and political democracy. The period began with a renewed commitment by the government of the United States to support social development in Egypt.

Shortly after his appointment, the minister announced in a press interview that he was going to be a candidate for a seat in the Parliament and urged his fellow cabinet members to do the same. Cabinet members in Egypt are not required to hold an elected office; the minister's bold announcement attracted considerable public attention, and several of his cabinet colleagues launched campaigns.

The minister's campaign speeches focused primarily on the conditions of education in Egypt, and his vision of a new education system that would prepare the country for the twenty-first century. The minister campaigned hard, using the media to build a high level of visibility among his constituency.

He attracted even more attention when he was elected and his fellow cabinet members were not. Something about the minister appeared almost daily on television, radio, or in the English and the national-language newspapers during the first six months after his election. As all his comments dealt with education, the public's consciousness of problems and opportunities of education in Egypt rose quickly.

The minister then proposed a National Conference on Education in which he sharpened his criticism of the existing system. The product of the conference was a list of 147 recommendations for change, some of which were explicitly contradictory. The empirical basis for the recommendations is unknown, as the conference documents make no reference to any studies or even statistics (other than rates of growth of enrollments) to support the assertions that are made.

Shortly before the national conference, the minister hired as his deputy a person trained in curriculum in the United States who had just finished a three-year period with the World Bank in Washington. The deputy was given responsibility for planning and organization of the process of reform and was in daily contact with the minister.

The deputy minister proposed the creation of a planning unit that would respond directly to the minister. It would prepare strategic plans for implementation of reform projects and would monitor all aspects of progress of the reform. The proposed changes would have required a major change in the structure of the Ministry of Education. The political process to gain official approval for these changes, and budget for new positions, was estimated to require two or more years. In order to begin the planning process immediately, the minister obtained financial and technical assistance from USAID. USAID suggested the employment of BRIDGES project staff and funds for the required tasks. In March 1988, a BRIDGES-sponsored team came to Egypt to design the new education planning unit.

This was not the first contact between USAID-financed consultants and education planners in Egypt. Consultants from another organization worked in Egypt in 1984 and 1985 doing basic studies on repetition, developing a basic information system, and providing training in planning procedures. Beginning in July 1986, consultants from the BRIDGES project began working with the ministry on further improvements in the management information system. Assistance was provided in the design of new procedures and instruments for data collection and training was provided in the use of microcomputers for data entry and simple reporting. These tasks required field visits to several states and interviews with ministry and state-level education officials on current issues and problems of planning. Consultants, together with ministry staff, carried out interviews with all major officials (about forty) in the ministry on the decisions they make each year and the information required and used in making these decisions.

These interviews provided a great deal of information about perceptions of the current performance of the education system by ministry officials. Much of this information is contained in trip reports by consultants written in English. The reports include a fairly comprehensive critique of the performance of primary and secondary education in Egypt, but no attempt was made to carry out a systematic analysis and description of problems. In an early consultant's report it was noted that there appeared to be a great deal of sensitivity to discussions of policy issues, such as goals, patterns of inequity in allocation of resources, and inefficiencies in procedures. His report suggested that "to open the work with a full-blown 'sector analysis' would be the worst possible strategy of assistance; the analysis should be done cooperatively and over time" (Davis, 1986, 15).

The strategy chosen in 1986 was to develop a system of information, including procedures for information distribution and utilization, that would allow Egyptian officials to detect for themselves problems and accomplishments of their system. BRIDGES consultants at this time had relatively easy access to ministry staff in their offices.

Meanwhile, the deputy minister put together a staff of persons with little or no prior experience in the ministry. For example, his chief planner was seconded from the ministry of planning. The head of the curriculum reform unit was contracted from a university. His advisory board was made up of university professors and officials, representatives from other ministries in the government, and the directors general of planning and statistics in education.

THE SECTOR ANALYSIS

The consultants' contract with USAID specified a series of activities (about fifty activities were listed), among them technical assistance in research and evaluation. The latter activities would include:

(1) development of staff capacity; (2) educational sector assessment; and (3) nine subsector and policy evaluation studies.

With respect to the sector assessment, the contract stated that the contractor would provide a plan for implementation of the sector assessment within three months, including identification of critical policy issues to be addressed and data requirements.

The contract also specified that the contractor would be responsible for producing the final report in English.

The contractors' proposal included two pages on the sector assessment. It would be carried out following the guidelines in the IEES Sector Assessment Manual. The assessment would review existing published and unpublished material in Arabic and English on education in Egypt in order to identify goal statements, descriptions of organizational structure, finance and operation, and empirical studies of performance and outcomes. It would compile and synthesize existing databases with special attention to issues of access, internal efficiency and quality, and quality of learning outcomes. Detailed information would be collected on costs and finance with attention to possibilities for mobilization of local resources and cost recovery. The assessment team would include pertinent officials from the educational planning unit of the Ministry of Education and other government employees and consultants. Each of the external consultants would be paired with an Egyptian counterpart. Most of these would be planning unit employees.

Each stage of the assessment would be reviewed with cognizant Ministry of Education and USAID project coordinators. The proposal stated that its goal would be to have the assessment disseminated to both Arabic- and English-speaking audiences.

The following steps were taken to prepare for the assessment. Efforts were made to identify all published research in English on education in Egypt. Those few publications or dissertations that promised some overview of the education system were read and abstracted.

The second step was that a resident contractor staff in Egypt identified and recruited for participation in the assessment Ministry of Education employees and other persons who could serve as counterparts for external consultants. This proved to be a difficult task.

The next step was that discussions were held with USAID and planning unit officials, especially the minister's deputy, about their objectives for the sector assessment. Two meetings were held in the United States among external consultants to discuss the general objectives of a sector assessment and the specific objectives of the assessment in Egypt.

Two issues emerged as the date for the assessment came closer. The first was that there was some disagreement about objectives for the assessment. The minister's deputy pointed out that the plan for the reform had already been laid out. What was required was not an identification of the fundamental problems facing the education sector of Egypt, but the development of a set of procedures to implement the activities being formalized in the reform law. USAID agreed with this objective for the assessment but indicated that it was planning a new basic education project for several years hence, and therefore would like information and analysis that would identify possible activities for new projects. USAID also indicated that it would appreciate information that would evaluate the importance of its massive ongoing project in primary school construction.

Discussions with ministry officials and the deputy did result in a change in the themes to be covered by the assessment. The topical organization originally proposed for the final assessment report was changed to match more closely the organization of the Ministry of Education. Scopes of work for external consultants were rewritten to reflect these changes in the task.

The second issue was with respect to identification of counterparts for the external consultants. The resident advisors for the project were placed in offices with the National Education Research Center (NERC) and the newly created Education Planning Unit (EPU), physically separated (by about four kilometers) from the offices of the operating divisions (i.e., primary, secondary, teacher training, textbooks, and vocational–technical education) of the ministry. The consultants were encouraged by ministry officials to draw their counterparts from the professionals in these offices.

Only one of the staff of the NERC had basic skills in quantitative analysis. All the staff were trained either in psychological or anthropological methods of inquiry that did not require large samples and sophisticated measurement. Most of the twelve professionals were completing master's or doctoral degrees in Egyptian universities. They had taken courses in statistics but had never used them. There were no microcomputers in the NERC offices or anywhere else in the Ministry of Education (apart from the statistics department and the minister's office). The prior research product of the NERC consisted of studies of teachers' and students' attitudes with respect to Ministry of Education policies and programs.

Members of the NERC had limited or negative relationships with other ministry staff. Unlike regular ministry employees, few NERC staff had been trained in teacher colleges. They were expected to pursue graduate studies in one of the social sciences, and they were paid salaries equivalent to the salary schedule of university faculty, significantly higher than their ministry colleagues.

NERC and EPU employees commented to the external advisors that they already had a full load of responsibilities, and that in the past they had been given extra compensation for participation in short-term activities not included in their job descriptions. They demonstrated little interest in the kinds of issues that the assessment was intended to study.

No formula was ever found to provide extra compensation to NERC staff without violating USAID guidelines. Nor was it possible to locate any other education research group in Egypt. This was because the consultant team had limited contacts and time and because the minister's deputy discouraged direct contacts with the universities.

In the meantime, the date for initiating the sector assessment approached. No suitable counterparts were found among staff of the operating divisions of the ministry. NERC and EPU staff were instructed by their superiors to cooperate with the assessment. Also, the team hired as a local consultant an economist trained in Great Britain, who worked on a freelance basis.

IMPLEMENTATION OF THE ASSESSMENT

Work on the assessment began October 15, 1989 with a meeting of all the participants. The team that was assembled included thirteen staff members from the NERC and EPU, one other local consultant, and eleven external consultants. Of these, four were resident advisors. Four of the eleven external consultants had prior experience in education in Egypt. One was fluent in Arabic.

The minister's deputy appeared briefly at the first meeting to welcome the consultants, but left without providing any specific instructions for the assessment. The assessment team leader, who had participated in several assessments in other countries, described the usual objectives of an assessment, and the procedures followed. Team members were provided with copies of the forty-two projects developed for the reform and copies in English of several speeches by the minister describing the objectives of the reform. Several hours were spent discussing the overall strategy for the team's work, procedures to be used, and deadlines.

Team members were encouraged to spend the first two weeks of their four-week assignment collecting information about the education system. They were invited to make use of a small library of documents and previous studies that had been collected from the ministry, from USAID offices, and some publications brought from the United States, including two sector assessments from other countries. They were encouraged to make contact with officials in the Ministry of Education's operating divisions. The Egyptian counterparts were asked to serve as translators where necessary. Team members were asked to make reports of their interviews and other activities; the team leader scheduled weekly meetings.

The team leader and the chief of party for the resident advisors also met with the steering committee that had been organized by the minister's deputy. The committee, chaired by the deputy, included: the director of the EPU; the undersecretary for Planning (previously head of the Statistics Department); the vice dean of a faculty of education in a leading university; the acting director of the Center for Curriculum Development (another USAID-funded project also located outside the operational divisions of the Ministry of Education); and the director of the Center for Higher Education Research (seconded from the NERC to head this new organization set up by the minister). The steering committee asked to review plans for the assessment including proposed interviews, initial drafts, final drafts, and recommendations resulting from the chapters of the report.

Three problems surfaced in the first two weeks of the work of the team. The first problem was that external consultants found it difficult to arrange and carry out interviews with Ministry of Education officials in the operating divisions. Several factors contributed to this difficulty, but principally telephone communications between the NERC and EPU offices and the rest of the Ministry of Education were limited and unreliable.

A second problem was that NERC staff increasingly found it difficult to participate with external consultants in arranging and carrying out interviews. This left the consultants essentially unable to communicate with educators outside that limited number that could speak English. Consultants found themselves limited to interviews with university-trained academics and high-level ministry officials. Efforts to engage NERC staff more fully, through joint planning of activities or offers of training in research or data analysis, were not successful.

A third problem was that several of the less-experienced external consultants, discouraged by difficulties of communication and transportation, began to reduce their efforts to gather information. One of the external consultants arrived in Egypt with the outline of his report essentially written. He said that he could tell immediately the nature of the problems facing the education system of Egypt and proceeded to write his report. Another of the consultants relied exclusively on a single, English-speaking informant for all his information and judgments about the education system. A third consultant spent most of his time analyzing on his personal computer a set of data he had obtained in the first days of the assessment.

By the end of the first two weeks, however, it was possible to share with the steering committee some of the initial findings and conclusions of the assessment team. This was carried out in the form of a brief, two-page listing in English of the major findings and conclusions, and a verbal presentation that included use of charts showing projected enrollment flows given different assumptions about promotion and repetition rates. For the most part, the meeting was dominated by the deputy, who made suggestions with respect to specific issues that should be addressed.

External consultant members of the assessment team insisted that they be invited to meetings with the steering committee, or that the steering committee attend their meetings. The committee refused both suggestions but the deputy did attend another meeting of the team and spoke at length about his and the minister's objectives for the education reform. He described the forty-two projects that he had designed (prior to the arrival of the consultants) to implement the reform.

The effect of this meeting was to redefine the purpose of the sector assessment. The deputy asked that the assessment investigate and specify ways in which the reform plan could be carried out. The assessment would identify key obstacles to implementation and specify ways to overcome these obstacles. The assessment document would be used as an implementation plan.

As work continued on the assessment, it became clear that there would be little or no opportunity to engage staff of the Ministry of Education in preparation of the various chapters. Also, members of the NERC and the EPU had less and less time to spend with their foreign counterparts. Efforts to prompt discussion of chapters during weekly meetings yielded little.

All chapters of the assessment were completed in draft form by November 15, with the exception of chapters on higher education and the economics of education. The chapters were reviewed and critiqued by the assessment team leader and returned to the authors for revision. By December 1, the team members had returned edited versions of all chapters, including the higher education chapter but excluding the economics of education chapter, and a summary chapter had been prepared.

With the exception of the observations made in the chapter on management, the assessment was not particularly critical of the education system of Egypt. The problems identified were ones that the ministry and USAID had themselves made on previous occasions.

The chapter on management of implementation, however, provided a detailed critique of the organizational and procedural shortcomings of the central bureaucracy of the Ministry of Education. The chapter ended with a prediction that the ministry would resist change.

IMPACT OF THE ASSESSMENT

Highlights of the draft were discussed with the minister. He asked for a translation of the summary of the assessment, and the chapters on the policy framework of the reform, basic education, and management issues in implementation of the reform. Response to the material translated into Arabic came from the minister within three weeks. He proposed minor changes in wording in several of the chapters. All the changes proposed had the effect of softening criticism of the existing operation of the education system, and of providing a more favorable prognosis of the implementation of the reform. Verbal agreements to changes were obtained from the authors.

At this time, the minister proposed to the chief of party of the consultant team a meeting of the steering committee and the directors of the curriculum reform unit and the policy research unit to discuss the translated chapters and the summary with their authors. Included in the group of authors were six Egyptian officials, five of whom were members of the NERC or the EPU. The chief of party submitted a memo to the director of the NERC reporting on the minister's request and proposing that the meeting be held within the unit.

There was no immediate response to the request. Meanwhile, the chief of party and the head of the assessment team were asked to make a presentation of the report to the assessment steering committee, who made brief comments about various chapters. Members of the committee were eager to know how the report had been received by the minister. On several occasions, the director of the NERC was asked when a meeting would be possible. He was unable to promise a specific date, claiming that staff were not available on one occasion and that the minister had not authorized distribution of the version of the report in Arabic on another occasion.

In the meantime, the minister of education asked the chief of party to prepare a summary version of the report in Arabic that could be printed in an internal bulletin of the Ministry of Education. The summary was written and translated and sent to the minister within two weeks, but it was never published. No one besides the minister ever admitted to having seen the summary statement, and the minister brushed aside the question in meetings with the chief of party.[1]

Apart from minor suggestions for revision (e.g., change of dates and correct names for offices) the only substantive reactions to the assessment report came from the minister. Each of the chapters of the report included a list of additional studies to facilitate the implementation of the reform. The minister culled from the chapters the fifteen studies that would be most important to him and asked the chief of party to indicate which of these would be of highest priority and how they should be carried out. This request from the minister led to a series of meetings between consultants and staff of the NERC. The minister's list of topics was shortened and recombined into five major topics. The minister gave his approval of this revised list of topics, and funding was secured from USAID.

It was not possible, however, to carry out these studies with the participation of the NERC. Staff members professed interest in the topics but argued that they should receive extra compensation—the research work would be done in addition to their regular duties. USAID officers adamantly opposed any additional payments on the grounds that this was contrary to USAID policy. The relationships between the consultant team and the NERC became increasingly tense.

In June 1990, the minister decided to move the EPU to the main building of the Ministry of Education. The position of undersecretary of educational planning was created. All the consultants moved into the ministry building.

The secretariat of educational planning was given three directorates—information (or statistics), planning, and research. As the information and planning units already existed, their directors continued in place. The research director, a former head of a teacher training college, was appointed by the minister. There was no research staff.

Given a lack of staff and no possibility of working with researchers at the NERC, the consultants decided to go outside the ministry for assistance. They proposed to invite the participation of universities in carrying out pilot studies that would provide some training for fledgling researchers hired into the ministry and which would provide consultants with professional counterparts.

The new undersecretary was asked to review the research topics and suggested some changes in the sequence in which studies would be carried out. Requests for proposals were prepared for eight topics. Each of the requests for proposals described the research problem, specified the kind of information required in the form of research questions, indicated the methods that might be used, asked for a written report and a conference presentation, specified the deadline for completion of the study, and specified a level of compensation.

Proposals for all eight topics were submitted by university professors and were reviewed by the undersecretary and staff. Five of the studies were completed within the specified time period—the end of October. Several meetings were held with the researchers to clarify the interests of the planning unit, suggest procedures, and ask for clarification of findings. The meetings brought the researchers together, and to the Ministry of Education, for the first time.

The findings of the five reports were summarized in brief and in the form of charts and graphs. In early November, the director of the research unit, together with the chief of party, presented the findings to the minister. He urged continuation of the research activities, with particular attention to the issue of private tuition and the identification of most-effective teaching practices. The minister asked the research director to prepare proposals on how to study those issues.

In an effort to insure the utility of the research to be carried out, the research director organized a meeting to which he invited representatives from all primary and lower secondary divisions of the ministry. Ten persons attended and provided suggestions as to what they would like to know to improve their work. Also, they validated the results of the pilot studies on private tutoring and teacher practices. Participants in the meeting asked to be informed of progress on the research. Also, they noted that this was the first time in their long years in the ministry that they had discussed research on ways to improve schooling.

Field work on a national sample survey study of determinants of school achievement began in March 1991. Work on a sample survey of parent, student, and teacher involvement in private tutoring began in June 1991. The final report on the school achievement study was delivered in October 1993, translated into Arabic, and circulated by the Ministry of Education. The tutoring study did not reach the final report stage.

DISCUSSION

This case is an illustration of an education sector assessment and of the importance of identifying and communicating with stakeholders at the outset of research and analysis.

The case illustrates that some contexts are not very supportive of open dissemination of information which might lead to questioning official policies. Communication between the sector assessment team and a larger group of stakeholders seems to have been prevented by the minister and his deputy. The process of preparing the assessment provided few opportunities for the team of advisors to gain the trust of national counterparts. Characteristics of the organization of the ministry, including poor horizontal communication, interdepartmental rivalries, and inadequate staff compensations and professionalism, constrained the opportunities for collaboration between national staff and their counterparts. The sector assessment was completed, but who learned from it? What did the assessment team learn from their counterparts and from local conditions in Egypt? What did Egyptian educators and stakeholders learn from the assessment? In the context of an authoritarian bureaucracy it is possible that senior officials at the top may have seen the assessment as being interested in inopportune questions, hence the emphasis the deputy minister placed on changing the terms of reference of the assessment to provide a plan to implement the already decided education reform.

NOTE

1. It should be noted, however, that during this period the only publication of information about the reform was in newspapers, generally through interviews with the minister. No systematic attempt was made to inform either the ministry nor the general public about details of the reform as a plan or as a process. In 1991, the minister published a personally authored book describing his ideas for the reform in English and Arabic.

Chapter 9

Conducting an Education Policy Survey in Honduras

This case illustrates how it is possible to involve decision makers in the initial design phase of research. This involvement can contribute to a fuller understanding by external researchers of the context in which the research will be carried out. Also, it contributes to the development of relationships of trust and, later, ownership of the research results by the decision makers.

In November 1990, the USAID mission to Honduras approached the HIID headquarters of the BRIDGES project to help them and the Ministry of Education to better understand the problem of primary grade repetition in that country.

Three years earlier, USAID had designed a project to improve the quality of primary education. This project had aimed at reducing repetition rates through a number of interventions, including the provision of specially designed textbooks to children in public primary schools. Two years into the project, however, preliminary feedback indicated that repetition rates were not changing. A new director of the office of Human Resource Development in USAID questioned the apparent failure of the project to reduce repetition rates. The director could not understand why a multimillion dollar project had been launched to solve a problem (i.e., repetition) without adequate research to identify the causes of the problem. The apparent failure of the project to reduce repetition rates suggested that a study was needed to better understand the conditions leading to repetition.

The BRIDGES project was a USAID-funded project which had successfully conducted a number of education research studies in several continents. Because of this experience, the USAID mission to Honduras approached the director of the project to request the design and implementation of a small study about why children repeated in Honduras. Only limited funds were available when the initial contact was made. As a consequence it was decided to follow a two-step strategy: (1) to begin with a pilot study which would identify promising policy variables and allow BRIDGES staff to develop a design and a set of instruments; and (2) to launch a second study should additional funds become available, using a larger probabilistic sample. This study would follow the experience of BRIDGES in Egypt, Pakistan, and Thailand, where it had carried out studies using samples of 500 schools, 1,000 teachers, and more than 10,000 students tested in several grades and subjects.

Because the USAID mission did not obtain the funds for the second stage of this strategy during the life of the BRIDGES project, only the smaller pilot study was implemented. The first task for BRIDGES was to negotiate with USAID the need to have the study serve a purpose for the Ministry of Education and also to have the direct participation of Honduran counterparts in the design and implementation of the research.

Two persons were assigned by the minister as counterparts to the study. They were the director and her deputy of the evaluation unit of the basic education project implemented by the ministry with funding from USAID.

In preparation for the study, BRIDGES contacted an education planner at UNESCO's regional office. This planner had a long-standing interest on the issue of grade repetition in the region. Staff from Harvard spent a day with the planner discussing possible issues to be investigated in the study and exploring hypotheses which could be used to design the study. At the same time, HIID staff undertook a review of the literature on repetition using the resources cited in two clearinghouses—ERIC, covering educational research in the United States; and REDUC, covering educational research in Latin America. This preparatory work informed the research team of the state of the art on grade repetition in Latin America and elsewhere.

PROCEDURE OF THE RESEARCH

In February 1991, an HIID staff member went to Honduras to coordinate the study. In addition to him, the research team included a person who had been a consultant to HIID in several projects and two Honduran counterparts. In Honduras preparation for the study began with interviews with ministry officials ranging from the minister and vice-minister to school supervisors, principals, and teachers. The purpose of these interviews was to understand the views of these groups with regards to repetition, to find out to what extent they perceived it as a problem, and to discover what the causes were to which they attributed it. Also, the research team wanted to familiarize themselves with the frames of mind of these groups and with the type of language they used to analyze education problems. The objective was to know how much was already known about the problem and to get a sense of the kinds of hypotheses that should be used in designing the study, as well as a sense of the type of evidence and language that should be used in communicating with this group once the study was finished.

A number of issues came up at these interviews which allowed researchers and policy makers to get to know each other better and to be more responsive to each others' needs. For instance, one of the concerns of the minister of education was that the report would take too long to be useful during his tenure. The consultants offered to have a draft report with recommendations in less than five months. When ministry staff understood that the researchers wanted to obtain candid interviews with teachers, officials facilitated access to the schools without intervention or presence of the school supervisors.

All staff in the human resources office of USAID were interviewed and the education officer accompanied the research team in some of the initial interviews with ministry staff. During this consultation with public officials the USAID official asked several times, "When are you actually going to begin the study?" In the official's eyes, this initial set of interviews with decision makers and implementors of education policy was not a part of the study.

Using the results of the preparatory design described and the results of the interviews, the research team prepared a theoretical model of repetition. This model emphasized those variables that reflected actions that could be taken by the Ministry of Education or by teachers in classrooms.

Because resource constraints indicated that it would be possible to work with only a small sample of schools, the study focused on rural primary schools, where national statistics indicated that the prevalence of grade repetition was higher. The sample drew students from two grades that seemed critical on the basis on national statistics—first and third grade. An intentional sample of forty schools was chosen (high and low repetition) in four districts of rural Honduras. The key information to be obtained included whether children were repeating, their achievement in a reading ability test, and interviews with teachers, principals, children, and parents. Information covered all the variables specified in the model elaborated on the basis of interviews and the literature review. The design overspecified the model with variables because this phase was seen as the first phase of a two-step process. One of the research goals was to narrow down the variables in the model to the best predictors, to be used in a large-scale second step of the survey.

A group of teachers was hired and trained to collect information. Principals, teachers, and all students in selected grades were interviewed, as well as the parents of half the students. Questionnaires and interviews were designed with ministry collaboration, including the two ministry staff who were members of the research team, and with feedback from the teachers who would work as interviewers. Once instruments were field tested, data were collected in March 1991 in forty schools in the selected departments.

Data were computerized, cleaned, and analyzed in a record period of three months. The deadline for completion of the report was taken very seriously; the analysis was designed to fit within the time constraints. The objective was to present a report in a timely fashion to the ministry. This meant that the researchers had to concentrate on the main line of analysis with most direct relevance for policy. The Honduran counterparts came to Harvard to participate in the analysis. The UNESCO planner also joined the team briefly during this period.

DISSEMINATION OF FINDINGS

A number of products were prepared to present the findings of the study. They included a final report with an executive summary, a shorter version of the study and a summary for wider dissemination, a slide-show presentation summarizing the findings and policy recommendations, and a press release. A Geographic Information System presentation was prepared to illustrate the impact, at the national level, of some of the policy recommendations of the study, such as targeting multigrade schools for training and appointment of additional teachers. A coordinator was hired to arrange presentation of findings to key audiences in Honduras.

Prior to presenting these findings, drafts of the report were circulated among senior officials in Honduras for feedback. These drafts were read, and they facilitated more informed discussion sessions. In June 1991, the Harvard team, counterparts, and UNESCO planner went to Honduras to participate in five presentations and discussions of the findings and recommendations with the following key audiences:

1. High-level decision makers. These included the minister and vice minister of education, the president's advisor on social policy, and other key senior government officials.

2. School supervisors and other Ministry of Education personnel

3. Ministry's Center for Research on Curriculum and Instruction. They were responsible for developing new textbooks and for organizing teacher training programs to implement the new curriculum.

4. Members of the research community, teacher unions, and the press

5. USAID personnel

All reports were written in Spanish, with the exception of a summary report in English for USAID staff and of a final report written after these presentations.

The study summarized its recommendations in the following seven key areas:

1. Increase in-service training for teachers in classroom management, including techniques for multigrade classrooms

2. Develop instructional materials that permit teachers to provide differentiated instruction

3. Increase the number of teachers in small schools to reduce the number of multigrade classrooms

4. Improve the ability of teachers to identify students with learning difficulties and establish remedial programs to reduce the failure rate of these students

5. Provide training to encourage teachers to raise their expectations for all students

6. Provide preschool experiences that improve students' learning capacity

7. Continue to carry out research that identifies problems that can be resolved by ministry action

IMPACT OF THE RESEARCH

The ministry has taken steps to implement these seven recommendations. The most significant one was to make multigrade schools, particularly those with fewer teachers, a priority for new teacher appointments and for teacher training. In spite of the fact that a different political party won the presidential elections with consequent changes in the Ministry of Education, attention to the problem of repetition, and the priority in multigrade schools, has continued.

Perhaps one of the most significant consequences of this activity is that a group of local university researchers participated, many of them for the first time, in the various policy studies which were commissioned by the redesigned project to improve basic education. This established new relationships between the university community and policy makers in the country.

Also, as a result of the mid-term evaluation of the basic education project, USAID decided to redesign and rebid the project. The new design called for a number of studies following the same format and process used by the HIID team in this study of repetition. As part of this project the local teacher training university has been contracted to do follow-up studies to look at the determinants of student failure and dropout.

This study of repetition served as a model which illustrated to the ministry that it was possible to have information generated from analysis emphasizing policy variables and that it was possible to have successful partnership with university-based analysts. Senior ministry personnel also learned that some of their fears about the dialogue sessions structured to discuss the research with different stakeholder groups (i.e., teacher unions) were unfounded, and that this exchange facilitated further negotiations between unions and ministry authorities.

This experience ended with a paradox for the Harvard team. Two days prior to the team's return to Honduras to present the report, the vice minister of education called HIID requesting that the results of the study not be disseminated to the different groups that had been invited for dialogue sessions. The prior experience of the ministry with studies and reports was that they were given to the most senior authorities, and that these authorities decided how much should be disclosed to others. Most prior reports funded by USAID had been written in English, so this automatically limited access to their content. The problem with this report is that it was written in Spanish. HIID was proposing to bring several hundred copies for distribution and discussion with several hundred people. This was a new scenario for the ministry and the uncertainty about the political ramifications of this strategy created fear.

As the Harvard team was not agreeable to censoring some of the findings from the public presentations, the team was invited to come to Honduras for one day to make presentations to the senior leadership of the ministry. After that meeting the minister decided to authorize the rest of the scheduled sessions but without endorsing the report or its recommendations.

As the consultants finished their last presentation, the private secretary of the minister called them to an emergency meeting. A car was sent to insure their immediate arrival at the minister's cabinet. There they were met by the minister and a delegation of the national press. The minister thanked the research team publicly for their contribution to the development of education in Honduras and gave each member of the research team a diploma in beautiful calligraphy stating his gratitude. The press took numerous pictures of the minister as he shook hands with each member of the research team. The next day several major newspapers reported that the minister endorsed a major study which had made pathbreaking advances to solve the problem of repetition. Newspapers, radio, and television reported the findings of the study, many of them quoting verbatim from the press releases and from the executive summaries.

Those diplomas hang on the walls of the consultants' offices as a reminder of the unexpected twists of the relationships between researchers and policy makers. The team stayed in touch with that minister for a while during his tenure, and he sent several delegations of visitors to Harvard University to learn firsthand about the study. He talked about the experience of the study at the regional meetings of ministers of education organized by the regional office of UNESCO. The study of repetition in Honduras entered the regional experience through several mechanisms. The results were cited in several publications on the subject of repetition and two other governments invited HIID to replicate similar studies in these countries.

DISCUSSION

This case illustrates that when research starts with the client in mind, dialogue can go a long way. The case combines the approaches discussed in Chapter 4—policy dialogue as communication and persuasion; and Chapter 5—policy dialogue as negotiation. In designing the study, the research team consulted extensively with policy makers and administrators. These interviews served to develop a context-specific model which served as the foundation to design the study and the data analysis plan. However, the task of conducting the study was primarily in the hands of the researchers, particularly the foreign researchers, as they had had more experience with similar activities and were perceived as the experts by their local counterparts. To present the results of the study, a strategy was designed to initiate dialogue with different groups of stakeholders, using various media—press releases, slide shows, summary, and copies of the report. This approach was innovative in Honduras and initiated a new relationship between research and policy making. The most direct impact of the study was to incorporate the issue of repetition and the constraints of single-teacher schools into the policy agenda, but the policy recommendations of the study did not have a direct impact on policy.

Chapter 10

Conducting an Education Policy Survey in Colombia

One of the functions of policy research is to define alternative solutions to critical issues. To do that, the research must generate definitive findings. It must show that A is related to B, or that changes in C will affect D. Research that generates no significant findings is useless to the policy maker, even if there are no relationships between the factors studied. This case illustrates the importance of building a strong constituency for the findings of a research study and of delivering clear-cut, positive findings.

In May 1991, the minister of education invited HIID to visit Colombia to explore a possible agreement to assist the newly elected government in the following educational activities:

1. Development of a statistical information system
2. Technical assistance to develop a system to measure school quality
3. Development of a training program for municipal personnel in school administration to facilitate the decentralization process which transferred school administration to municipal authorities
4. Design and implementation of a study of grade repetition

The study of grade repetition was somewhat of an afterthought in the initial negotiations of collaboration. The Harvard team was just completing the study of repetition in Honduras and brought it up as an example of an analytic activity which could support policy reform. The director of the ministry of planning and the vice minister of education liked the approach followed in Honduras and requested a similar study for Colombia.

In September 1991, HIID began activities in Colombia. A consultant met with senior staff in the Ministries of Education and Planning in order to develop a work plan. A significant change to the work plan from the earlier conversations which had taken place in May was the elimination of technical assistance to develop a system to measure school quality. The development of this system had been commissioned to Instituto Ser, a local think tank in social policy. This group and the technical personnel had not requested the assistance from HIID, and they perceived the proposal as an expression of lack of confidence by senior ministry staff in local consultants.

Technical staff in the ministry requested feedback about the achievement tests which they were developing. The Harvard consultants indicated that the tests were unlikely to be sensitive to the kinds of factors that are affected by Ministry of Education policies. This criticism was leaked to Instituto Ser as they prepared the test and was construed to suggest that the relationship would be one of competition rather than collaboration, diminishing further possibilities of collaboration with the study of grade repetition.

In October 1991, an HIID consultant arrived in Colombia to coordinate the study of grade repetition. Upon his arrival, he found that negotiations between HIID and the ministry had been delayed and that a contract had not yet been signed. Again, the vice minister of education brought up the need for coordination between the activities of Instituto Ser and those of HIID. The director of Instituto Ser indicated that collaboration would not be feasible given the advanced state of their project. This reinforced the perception of rivalry between the technical assistance activities of local teams and the Harvard team. For instance, a nationally representative sample had been drawn for the quality study, and Instituto Ser challenged the Harvard team to have an equally large and representative sample, something beyond the objectives of the original design and beyond the level of resources allocated for the activity. The vice minister suggested that HIID assist Instituto Ser with the analysis of the data, but this suggestion was rejected on the grounds that HIID had no particular expertise beyond that of the professionals of Instituto Ser.

While Instituto Ser and HIID concluded that they would not collaborate in the implementation of the studies, senior ministry staff continued expecting that coordination and collaboration would take place. A few months later, when it became obvious that Harvard was not collaborating in the analysis of the data collected by Instituto Ser, some senior staff in the ministry perceived this as a breach of contract by Harvard. This created an unfavorable climate for the study of repetition that was under way.

PROCEDURE OF THE REPETITION STUDY

The HIID consultant directing the study contacted a group of researchers at the research center of the Pedagogic University who had been working on the theme of automatic promotion. The vice minister, however, did not trust the technical competency of this team and created obstacles for their incorporation into the project.

At the end of October, the HIID consultant interviewed staff in several offices in the Ministry of Education to incorporate their concerns and needs for information into the study. A set of questionnaires was designed and field tested. Just as the instruments were ready, the minister and vice minister of education resigned, along with the person who had been assigned by the vice minister as counterpart for the study.

The new minister and vice minister had no particular interest in the study. Negotiations over the contract and the incorporation of the researchers from the Pedagogic University were further delayed. In spite of this, the study continued.

Field work began in March 1992 with participation from the Pedagogic University and from the evaluation unit in the ministry. Data were collected successfully, generating renewed interest in the ministry in the results of the study. Data were computerized in the ministry in about a month and were then taken to Harvard for analysis. From that moment, data analysis was split: Qualitative analysis was conducted by the researchers of the Pedagogic University and quantitative analysis took place at Harvard. A representative of the ministry was invited to participate in the analysis at Harvard, and the minister selected his personal secretary for this purpose. This choice of person alienated the technical divisions in the ministry that had collaborated with the study. Because this activity had not been anticipated in the work plan and budget, Harvard could not spend time collaborating with the researchers doing the qualitative analysis in the Pedagogic University. They felt left out of the project.

In the summer of 1992, the ministry requested a presentation of preliminary results of the study at a seminar in Colombia to discuss the quality of education. This meeting was attended by representatives from the World Bank, education researchers, and ministry staff. The analysis of the data was not yet completed and the presentation disappointed many of the participants in the seminar. This bad initial experience in dissemination diminished the interest in the study and the chances of further diffusion of the results of the study.

At a later date, the final results of the study were presented to the minister, vice minister, and senior ministry staff. These people did not find sufficient elements in the results to support policy change. Their criticisms to the study were as follows:

- The results of the study are inconclusive.
- The results of the study have no explanatory power.
- The study is based on data of very poor quality but with good recommendations which are not based on the data.
- The study did not include the qualitative analysis prepared by the local researchers that is perceived as lack of confidence in local capacity.
- It is felt that the results of the study are not up to the expectations generated by a university with Harvard's prestige.

In contrast to the limited dissemination activities organized by HIID, the team of the Pedagogic University carried out its own activities to disseminate the qualitative section of the study. They presented the study at a national symposium on education quality and at several meetings with the departmental secretaries of education. At these meetings the emphasis was on the results of the qualitative analysis, as the team had not participated in the quantitative analysis and did not understand these results well enough to present them appropriately. The Pedagogic University prepared a special report on repetition, addressed to primary school teachers. Some 26,000 copies of this report were printed but could not be distributed as intended because of lack of funds.

Among the factors which have been pointed out as limiting the impact of the study are the following:

- Only three copies of the final report were delivered to the ministry authorities. Many people who collaborated with the study never saw a final report.
- The researchers of the Pedagogic University did not receive a copy of the study.
- Harvard's final report did not acknowledge the participation of the researchers from the Pedagogic University.
- The private secretary of the minister who participated in the quantitative analysis at Harvard did not contribute to the dissemination of the results.

IMPACT OF THE STUDY

Within the Ministry of Education, the study had no impact on policy and was forgotten. All the ministry staff interviewed in 1994 in preparation for this case were unable to recall a single finding of the study. The theme of grade repetition, however, entered the debate about quality of education. The former director of evaluation in the ministry expressed that until the study was done, the theme of repetition had not been considered a problem related to education quality. This division had worked closely with the policy of automatic promotion but had centered it around the theme of student assessment as a problem of internal efficiency; the possibility that repeaters would indicate lack of opportunities to learn had not been considered.

A more significant impact took place among the community of education researchers, particularly in the Pedagogic University, who began to recognize the importance of policy-oriented research. Two of the researchers who participated in the study decided to pursue graduate studies in education policy at Harvard. One of them eventually became an advisor to the vice minister of education and, later, a senior official in the ministry. This person revived the repetition report, had it published by the ministry, and distributed it widely in the system.

Among the researchers who collaborated closely with it, the study generated a new sense of standards of quality. This group of researchers saw the study as an opportunity for technology transfer, and it learned by doing in the process of instrument design, sample selection, and data collection.

DISCUSSION

The repetition study in Colombia illustrates the importance of political mapping and stakeholder analysis at the initiation of research activities. The local think tank was a very important stakeholder who was alienated from collaborating in the task of informing policies in the Ministry of Education. At the same time, the Harvard team failed to build a constituency among Ministry of Education staff for this study.

Organizational and political dynamics in the Ministry of Education also created a challenging environment to conduct research. Poor communication between units, lack of trust of the senior authorities toward researchers in the Pedagogic University, and patronage in nomination of counterparts for trips overseas furthered existing cleavages, making it difficult to build dialogue toward a common vision about the problem of repetition.

The case illustrates how trust is built over time and shows the significance of all events in shaping a history of trust. The HIID team was drawn into presenting results of the study prematurely, undermining the credibility of the report, even after the analysis had been completed.

Chapter 11

Conducting a Participatory Sector Assessment in El Salvador

In the summer of 1993, HIID responded to a request for proposal from the USAID mission to El Salvador. It called for an assessment of the education sector aimed at identifying options and priorities for policy reform. HIID saw this request as an opportunity to open up the space for education policy discussions to a wide range of people with different political views. A long period of conflict in El Salvador had resulted in the resolution of political differences by use of high levels of violence. After this conflict there were few spaces left for political dialogue and negotiation.

In September 1993, a consultant from HIID arrived in El Salvador to coordinate the preparation of the assessment. The HIID proposal emphasized a highly participatory process to conduct the assessment. Twenty-two of the thirty-five technical advisors who wrote the assessment were citizens of El Salvador. Collaborating in the preparation of the assessment were two institutions with credibility among different political groups: a prestigious private university Universidad Centro Americana (UCA) that had been a source of criticism of government policies, and an education foundation set up by the business community Fundación Empresarial para el Desarrollo de la Educación (FEPADE). The Ministry of Education was a full participant. "The Ministry of Education was an important partner, with both officials and technical staff participating through many hours of interviews as well as information and logistical support. The Minister met with research teams every week for several hours from October to December" (Representative from UCA, in Reimers, 1995, 24).

Each of the technical groups conducting the ten studies that were part of the sector assessment organized focus groups to explore issues and conclusions regarding each subject analyzed in the assessment. For example, the group working on the nonformal education chapter organized a three-day seminar to which more than thirty representatives of nongovernment organizations (NGOs) active in nonformal education were invited to discuss the principal questions of that study.

At the beginning of the project, the coordinator of the HIID project had conversations with USAID and the Ministry of Education aimed at agreeing on the distinction between clients and sponsors of the activity. Harvard proposed that the clients would have to be key stakeholders for education reform in the country. USAID would be the sponsor but not the prime client for the project. This had implications for how project resources would be spent. For example, it meant that the final reports would be written in Spanish rather than in English, departing from usual practice in USAID-funded projects of this type. Also, it meant that the primary effort of the technical team would be in dialoguing with these stakeholders rather than with USAID staff. The director of the Office of Education in the USAID mission shared this vision and supported this approach.

A similar dialogue took place with the Ministry of Education. Given that there would be elections a few months after the completion of the assessment, it was agreed that the focus of the project should be on stimulating and supporting dialogue within a wider group of stakeholders on the directions for education reform. There was uncertainty about who would win the elections and, consequently, about who would be the education authorities in the upcoming government.

PROCEDURES OF THE STUDY

In coordination with UCA, FEPADE, USAID, and the Ministry of Education, HIID organized an advisory committee for the assessment. This committee included some fifty representatives of more than thirty organizations, including the Ministries of Education, Planning, and Finance, Congress, a formerly armed group in opposition to the government (the principal opposition force), the Chamber of Commerce and the association of exporters, the association of industrialists, teacher unions, public and private universities,

NGOs, and other relevant groups. The committee met with the professionals writing the chapters of the assessment every week between September and December 1993.

While it was made clear to the committee that the final report would be the responsibility of the technical teams, in practice the weekly meetings served two purposes. One purpose was that they helped the technical teams writing the assessment better understand the perspectives of the advisory committee for policy relevant analysis. At the same time, the members of the committee were better able to ground their discussion on concrete issues and evidence as these were advanced by the technical teams. "The final result was the outcome of a long process of exchange of ideas, or multiple rounds of feedback, of examining information from primary sources and experience, and of multiple drafts of each chapter" (President of FEPADE, in Reimers, 1995, 26).

After initial discussions with the advisory committee and after initial interviews with key staff in the Ministry of Education, it was agreed that the assessment would cover the following ten topics:

1. An overall synthesis
2. A study of the macroeconomic trends and the implications for human resource requirements
3. A study on the costs, benefits, and financing of education
4. A study on preschool and basic education
5. A study on secondary education
6. A study on technical and vocational education
7. A study on higher education
8. A study on nonformal education
9. A study on management education
10. A study on management and decentralization of education

The difficulties of bringing together to the same table participants who had taken different sides during the conflict should not be underestimated. Even though peace agreements had been signed almost two years prior to beginning the assessment, there had been no opportunities since, and for many years during, the war for pluralistic committees to discuss national policy issues. The participation in the activity of different institutions, such as the Ministry of Education, FEPADE, UCA, USAID, and Harvard University made the activity sufficiently interesting for different groups to agree to participate. Several of them indicated repeatedly that the reason why they agreed to participate is that the mix of sponsoring institutions suggested that there was not an ideological or party bias in the nature of the activity.

The organizers tried to maintain the content of the conversations in the same level above local politics. For example, at the first meeting one of the participants, a former leader of the armed opposition, suggested that before we could agree on a path for education reform the committee should agree on a vision of the new man for El Salvador. The Harvard study director replied that the objective was more modest—to find agreement on small problems of the education system, nuts and bolts kinds of issues.

At the time, some felt disappointed to find out that this committee would not tackle the big questions, such as the type of society that the education system would be building. Later on it became clear that some of the small problems were not so small, and that it was possible to find agreement on them without addressing the reasons why they were perceived as problems by various groups. For instance, all agreed that the fact that 15 percent of the children never entered first grade, and that one in four children among the poorest 20 percent of the population never entered school, were problems that needed urgent attention. In private conversations with members of the committee it became clear that access was seen as a problem for very different reasons by different political groups, but the groups concentrated on the problem and possible solution rather than on the reasons and the value systems by reference to which these were seen as problems.

Each chapter of the report was reproduced as a stand-alone document with its own executive summary to facilitate access to the information by specialized audiences. A special synthesis was prepared of the ten chapters using many graphics and visual displays. A computerized graphics presentation was prepared to facilitate the exposition of the summary and of each of the chapters in different meetings. A press release was prepared for meetings with the press.

PROCEDURES FOR DISSEMINATION

In January 1994, HIID, the UCA, and FEPADE conducted a series of workshops, endorsed by the advisory committee, to present and discuss the results of the assessment with key groups of stakeholders for education policy. A strategy was designed for dissemination of the findings of the assessment.

One of these meetings was with the presidential candidates, all of whom showed great interest in the subjects being discussed. The day after this meeting, the principal opposition candidate appeared in national news echoing some of the key themes and recommendations of the report. From that moment, education reform became a central issue in the electoral debate.

Another meeting was with senior officials in the Ministry of Education. As a result of this meeting, the minister decided to organize an eight-hour workshop to discuss the results of the assessment with key managers of the ministry. A meeting was held with 200 staff—proportionately, a small number in a ministry with 7,000 administrators—of the ministry, who came from the capital and from different regions of the country.

Also, meetings were held with the press, with the Chamber of Commerce and the private sector, with the public and university communities, and with the Ministry of Planning. Some 500 copies of the final report were distributed upon request. As a result of this demand, the editorial center of the UCA published 1,500 copies of the report in 1994.

IMPACT OF THE STUDY

Less than a month after the presentation of the results of the assessment, the minister of education announced a modification of the curriculum of secondary education, in line with the recommendations of the assessment. Also, the ministry began to implement a program of administrative decentralization along the lines suggested in the respective chapter of the assessment. A group of private businesses actively lobbied Congress using the respective chapter of the assessment as principal source of arguments. Their goal was to have Congress prepare the decree to implement a law that creates a national institute of technical training. They lobbied based on the recommendation of the assessment which proposes a coordinating and regulatory role for the state, and responsibility for actual delivery of the training for the private sector.

After the new government took office in the summer of 1994, the minister of education was asked to continue, an unusual move of administrative continuity in Latin America. Most of the staff in the ministry remained. The former director of planning, who had actively participated in the advisory committee, became the vice minister of education. Two of the most senior staff of the UCA who participated in the study were hired by the Ministry of Education as directors of research and of secondary education.

Some of the areas of policy reform which can be linked to the assessment include the following:

1. The ministry has made expanding access in rural areas a policy priority. New sections and new teacher appointments are being made, giving priority to the rural areas.

2. The ministry has begun to experiment with school autonomy; on a pilot basis, schools will be given a modest fund which teachers, principals, and parents will destine to what they perceive as the greatest need to improve teaching effectiveness.

3. The ministry is making teacher training a priority area for the design of large education projects with funding from international development banks.

4. Administrative decentralization has continued, transferring responsibilities to the departments as suggested in the assessment. The Ministry of Planning finally approved this strategy in November 1994.

5. Parent and community participation has been fostered, not only involving them in decision making in the management of the school funds but establishing focus groups in communities to consult on education issues. The minister conducted a series of public fora to inform parents and the public at large about the conditions of schools and the main problems confronted by the education system. The ministry also conducted several focus groups to receive feedback from teachers.

6. Supporting innovations at the local level, the ministry is supporting a number of model schools with specially trained teachers to serve as trainers.

The content of the sector assessment was also used in negotiations between the government and the multilateral financial institutions to design education improvement projects.

Perhaps the most striking consequence of the assessment was that it released a process of public discussion of education issues. Several organizations in the country produced their own reports on the problems of the education sector and on possible solutions to these problems. All these organizations had participated in the advisory committee of the assessment, and some had direct participation in the technical team writing the assessment. A think tank on economic and social policy produced a policy brief on education and human resources and sponsored several paid pages in the national press about the problems and options to improve educational opportunities. The director of the social policy sector of this think tank, who was a consultant working on the chapter of administrative reform in the sector assessment, became a vocal spokesperson for education issues in several national fora.

The Salvadorean professionals who participated in the project were highly positive about the methodology. "Active participation by widely disparate groups in El Salvador has facilitated the analytical work and acceptance of its outcomes. A precedent-setting, much needed, national dialogue on education issues and policy is now underway in El Salvador" (Official from USAID, in Reimers, 1995, 36).

Through the participatory methodology the sector assessment became a process of pluralistic reflection, and an opportunity to consider options for education reform. The final report has an excellent content, insufficient in itself to launch a rapid change in the education system, but of critical value to impress in the highest levels of decision making in the country that education in El Salvador should have the highest priority, and that a change is necessary not just in the funds assigned to the sector, but in the systems, procedures, decentralization and general improvement of teaching." (President of FEPADE, in Reimers, 1995, 25–26)

The UCA produced, in addition to the publication of the sector assessment as a book, a special issue on education in a journal which regularly discusses social and economic topics. This issue drew directly from the chapters written by UCA staff in the assessment.

A think tank closely associated with the Christian Democratic Party produced two publications and sponsored a national forum of dialogue on education following the completion of the assessment. These publications drew on the assessment document. The senior person in charge of social policy in this center, who had participated in the advisory committee, said the meetings of the committee had worked as an advanced seminar generating much deeper understanding of education issues in the country. Similar comments were made by the person responsible for social policy in the think tank:

The participatory methodology permitted a valuable transfer of technology; it provided the persons involved with an opportunity for professional enrichment. The conceptual and analytic skills of the national teams were expanded through collaboration with international consultants who found in each working team a counterpart with information, a national perspective and a space for transfer of technology. In this way the study achieved the best of international assistance and generated conditions favorable to implementation of the specific recommendations. (Staff member from FUSADES, in Reimers, 1995, 31)

The education sector assessment in El Salvador served as an opportunity to establish new partnerships between university faculty and government officials; between the public and private sectors; and between political parties, the business community, religious organizations, and community groups. It stimulated a process of public dialogue about education and it opened new avenues to expand educational opportunities.

The selection of national institutions to work as technical counterparts was a great success. The partnerships HIID established with FEPADE, UCA and the various directorates of the Ministry of Education provided opportunities for participation from the outset. The configuration of an advisory committee with representatives of different sectors such as the teacher unions, the private sector, NGOs, also promoted levels of participation without precedent in the education sector in this country. (Minister of Education, in Reimers, 1995, 20)

DISCUSSION

This case illustrates some elements of the approach presented in Chapter 6 and the paramount importance of process in structuring opportunities for informed dialogue. The education sector assessment in El Salvador created opportunities for participation from a wide range of stakeholders. It established mechanisms for informed dialogue and for systematic exchanges between researchers and stakeholders. Technical analysis was designed to inform questions of stakeholders and analysis was informed by discussions of ongoing examination of evidence. The case illustrates that with participation comes ownership of the results of the research. It is interesting that, as in the consultation in Namibia, the coordinator of the assessment avoided getting into discussions about ultimate goals and concentrated instead on discussing specific education issues and activities. The comment of the president of FEPADE, stating that the analysis itself was not sufficient to make decisions, highlights the awareness generated in the dialogue surrounding the preparation of the assessment about the limits of technical rationality for decision making.

Chapter 12

Policy Dialogue as Organizational Learning in Paraguay

In May 1995, the Ministry of Education of Paraguay signed an agreement with HIID to receive technical assistance to increase the capacity of the Ministry of Education to use information for policy. The ministry requested that a first objective of the project would be to formulate a strategic plan for an education reform.

After several decades of military rule, Paraguay began the transition to democracy in 1989. One of the first acts of the transition regime was to appoint an advisory committee to an education reform. During the first regime of the transition, the frequent changes of the minister, and the fact that many of the senior staff had worked in the ministry during many of the years of the dictatorial regime and were perceived by the reform commission as ambivalent toward the need to reform education, made advances in the change process difficult. In 1993 the first elected government in decades in Paraguay reaffirmed its commitment to improving education. The new minister of education changed most of the senior staff in the ministry with people more favorable to reform. Projects to improve the quality of primary and secondary education were initiated with support of the Inter-American Development Bank and of the World Bank, respectively.

When the HIID team arrived in Paraguay to conduct negotiations about the terms of reference of the project in January 1995, the ministry gave the impression of being in disarray. While there was public acceptance of the idea of education change and while the projects financed by the banks were supporting some concrete inputs to improve quality and access to school, every unit in the ministry seemed to be working in isolation from the rest. A reform to change the curriculum was underway, controlled largely by the curriculum department. There was no impact on the work of the teacher training department, for example, and there were few links of coordination with the departments of primary and secondary education, under whose authority worked all of the school supervisors. Also, while there seemed to be public support for the idea of a reform of the education system, few people seemed to know what the reform was about. While the idea of a reform seemed to receive much lip service by internal and external stakeholders, few, including members of the advisory reform commission and the senior managers of the ministry, could formulate a vision of the reform. The reform commission had produced a couple of documents stating the goals of the reform, largely to contribute to the consolidation of democracy and to increase productivity, but there were no specific programs identified which would operationalize those objectives.

PROCEDURES OF THE STUDY

In this case, the Harvard advisors resisted the demands of the ministry to produce a strategic plan and a series of studies. Instead, they focused on developing institutional capacity to produce that plan and to generate research-based knowledge. They proposed to structure the project to provide technical support to four centers in the ministry, namely, a strategic dialogue group which would be created, a policy analysis unit, the planning unit, and a research unit.

The Strategic Dialogue Group. This group was formed at the start of the Harvard project. It included all senior members of the Ministry of Education—all directors of the department, about twenty, plus the vice minister and the minister of education. It also included all members of the advisory committee of the reform.

The goal of the group was to develop a common language and a shared vision among the leadership of the education system about the goals of the reform, and about specific projects which could be implemented to support it. This group agreed to meet once a week for several hours every week. At the first meeting, the objectives of the group work and a methodology were agreed upon. It was agreed that a facilitator would be brought in for the first several sessions to assist this group in establishing frank conversations and in reaching agreements. During the first meetings the group also negotiated the themes which would be examined during the following several months and a procedure to discuss them.

For each theme a background paper would be discussed. The themes included: primary education, secondary education, technical education, teacher training, adult education, special education, higher education, bilingual education, management and decentralization, finance, and scenarios about the future in economics, politics, and demography.

The preparation of the papers was coordinated by the policy analysis unit. Each paper was in charge of a couple of people, including the director of the department most directly concerned with the topic and a member of the advisory committee of the reform. Other participants included the four members of the policy analysis unit—created on an ad hoc basis and reporting directly to the minister—and consultants brought in by Harvard.

The dialogue group discussed several reports of research prepared by an education research group established in the ministry at project start and some reports analyzing statistical data prepared by the planning unit. The meeting of the strategic dialogue group alternated between discussions of the topics mentioned and participation in a training management program designed by Harvard.

One of the agreements established at the outset in the strategic dialogue group was that efforts would be made to inform the discussions with evidence. The role of the policy analysis unit, the planning unit, and the research unit would be to provide that evidence.

The Policy Analysis Unit. This unit was established to coordinate the preparation of the issue papers with more expedience than the planning unit could while still attending to its usual business. It was felt by many senior ministry administrators and members of the advisory commission for the reform that the planning unit's capacity was very weak to conduct this task. While efforts would be made to build that capacity over time, we considered it necessary to establish this ad hoc group that would coordinate the discussions and work of the strategic dialogue group. In so doing, the planning function was shifted from the planning unit to all the senior leadership of the ministry.

The Research Unit. The research unit was established in the largest and most important teacher training institution in the country. A group of eight professionals was deployed to work, along with Harvard consultants, in the preparation of several studies. At the outset it was decided that the objective of this unit was twofold: to build capacity to conduct research and to prepare reports that would provide formative feedback about the implementation of the reform to the senior managers of the Ministry of Education.

Two years prior to the establishment of the strategic dialogue group, the ministry had begun a curriculum reform of primary education. Basic education had been extended from six to nine grades.

A new curriculum had been designed for the first three grades. Textbooks had been prepared reflecting this curriculum. A pilot project to teach Guarani-speaking children in their mother tongue had been initiated in some 400 schools. The implementation of these programs followed a traditional top-down approach. To refer to the implementation of the curriculum, ministry staff talked about the technical delivery of the curriculum. This language reflected the hierarchical approach that was being used. Staff from the Ministry of Education, primarily from the Department of Curriculum, crisscrossed the country attending meetings in which teachers of first grade were brought in groups of 500 to 1,000. There, during a nine-day period, the curriculum experts explained the rationale for the curriculum change and reviewed the textbooks with the teachers. It was expected that this series of pep talks and presentations of the textbooks would enable the teachers to go back to their classrooms and shift the way they had taught for decades to a more student-centered approach, based on constructivist psychology. Without feedback on the success of this strategy, the same approach was followed to deliver the curriculum to the teachers of grade two in the second year of the implementation of the reform.

At the outset, the research group created in the teacher training institution defined its role as the provider of a voice for teachers in the process of implementation of the reform. The study was designed in consultation with the members of the strategic dialogue group, who were seen as the main audience for the report. The strategic dialogue group expressed much interest in how things were going with the implementation of the reform and in the views that teachers had about the reform. The first study conducted by the research group was a consultation with some 200 teachers, in focus groups around the country, to hear their views about the new curriculum and the strategy used to implement it. Teachers appeared to favor change in education and the general orientation of the new curriculum. However, in their view the strategy used to implement the change left much to be desired. Just as they began to be motivated for the change, they felt that the experts took off and that they were left in schools where no one else had heard about the changes. They had no one with whom to discuss them. Some teachers felt the trainers assumed they were stupid or ignorant, treating them like children or trainees without experience. They sensed the approach used to train them contradicted the postulates of the new curriculum. They were being told to use participatory methods, to help students construct their own knowledge, and to be centered in their students by trainers whose practice contradicted that message, who talked all the time, who showed no interest in the experiences of those they were training, and who did not encourage participation.

The presentation of the report of this study to the strategic dialogue group was followed by a long and cold silence in a group which had grown accustomed to lively exchanges and heated debates of the main problems and options for reform in the different subsectors of the education system. After a while, several participants began to express that these results confirmed their fears and intuitions based on hearsay and on personal visits to schools. There was time to change the approach to implementing the reform. The report was most resisted by the director of curriculum. While the report made some general recommendations on alternatives to organize the implementation of the new curriculum, a new way to do this was created collectively as the discussions of the strategic dialogue group unfolded. The alternative proposed was a significant departure from recent practice. It proposed to establish groups of teachers at the local level—circles of learning—in which teachers and principals together would review the new curriculum, teacher guides, and textbooks; would discuss ways to implement these changes in their classrooms; and would meet periodically to assess the progress of the change. The experts who would be hired would no longer be from the department of curriculum, but would include local experts from teacher training institutions or supervisors. The ministry would assess from time to time how the circles of learning were working and would make adjustments as necessary. The research group was asked to follow up the implementation of the circles of learning, and three additional studies followed in which researchers observed those circles, interviewed teachers and facilitators, and continued to inform the strategic dialogue group. Thus began the implementation of the new curriculum in grade three, with a 180-degree change in strategy, developed and owned by all senior staff of the ministry. The research group was ecstatic that choosing to portray the voice of the teachers could have such significant impact in official policy.

The follow-up studies of the circles of learning suggested that the relatively standardized prescription proposed by the new curriculum constrained the discussions at the local level. The research group conducted a study aimed at promoting local discussions of what was necessary to develop a school improvement plan. This research consisted of seven case studies of schools reputed to be particularly effective in some respect. One was a school with a very good bilingual education program, another was a school with excellent relations to the community, and other schools were good in other ways. The researchers conducted brief observations and interviews in the schools and wrote up a report which summarized twenty-two common traits in these schools. Some referred to how schools were managed, others to how classrooms were managed, and others to relations between the school and the community. The report was written as a guide for discussion in circles of learning and was distributed to all teachers. This generated a process of discussion in schools about what it meant to be effective in their particular context.

Other studies conducted during the first year by the research unit included a study of effective circles of learning and a large probabilistic school survey to examine the implementation of the different inputs of the reform and to solicit the views of teachers regarding textbooks, circles of learning, and so on.

The strategic dialogue group followed the preparation of each of these studies with great interest. This encouraged the researchers to continue on a tight schedule designed to deliver prompt reports; they knew actions would follow that would take these results into account. The researchers could not anticipate what changes would be implemented on the basis of their recommendations, for their findings would be given meaning after much discussion and integration with other pieces of information reviewed by the strategic dialogue group.

After six months of these discussions, the strategic dialogue group had shared a vast amount of information about the education system and about the initiatives under way to improve it. They had reached some consensus on further changes to be implemented. Many members of the group expressed that these discussions had helped them see the whole picture of education and that they had a better sense of integration and of how their particular work related to what others did. It is noteworthy that the minister attended very few of the meetings of the group. At the beginning, this created anxiety among some of the directors, who kept asking, "Who is going to make decisions based on our discussions?" With time, it became clear that decisions were being made as reflected in changes in the direction in each department, consistent with the discussions of the strategic dialogue group. Policy change was being formed without being announced or decided by the minister.

At this point, the group felt it was ready to engage a larger public in these discussions. Though this had been an objective from the start, the group had agreed to postpone these meetings until they had developed a proposal in sufficient detail to discuss it with others. The protracted discussions combined with the training received by senior Ministry of Education staff seemed to have given them the sense of self-efficacy to engage in dialogue with other social leaders. In preparation for these discussions all members of the strategic dialogue group, along with teacher-union leaders, participated in a workshop on negotiation and conflict resolution. Their ratings of this activity were so positive that they decided to extend it to all school supervisors, local education authorities, and local union leaders.

After this training, a series of twenty roundtables were conducted in which approximately thirty leaders participated in discussions of a proposal for education change. This 100-page document synthesized more than 2,000 pages of analyses reviewed by the strategic dialogue group in their weekly meetings. The document presented a diagnosis of the main problems facing the education system and proposed a broad agenda for reform. The roundtables included participation of members of Congress, businessmen, political and union leaders, presidents of universities and private schools, school supervisors, mayors, governors, and religious and cultural leaders. Each group met between four and sixteen hours. Some participants in these groups organized other consultation sessions. All directors of the ministry held meetings with the staff in their departments. School supervisors were asked to organize meetings with teachers at the local level to discuss the proposal for change. The base document was summarized in a synthesis developed by a team of participants in the strategic dialogue group. About 3,000 copies of the document were distributed for discussion.

During a period of three months, members of the strategic dialogue group invited feedback to the proposal for change. The weekly meetings of the group during this period focused on the feedback they were receiving. On the basis of this feedback, a strategic plan was developed. This plan identified priority areas and programs and activities to implement an education reform. The plan was budgeted and used to obtain additional resources from the ministry of finance and from the private sector.

In this process of strategic planning developed in the Ministry of Education in Paraguay, what is of most interest is not that a plan was developed but that procedures were established for ongoing dialogue among managers at different levels within the ministry and for dialogue with stakeholders outside the ministry. The concurrent emphasis on dialogue, at the top and at the school level, as a means to reach agreement on the main problems and to design strategies for improvement produced synergistic effects which opened up opportunities for significant changes in the approach used to train teachers in a system accustomed to authoritarian rule and management.

About a year after the strategic dialogue group began to meet, a small military group attempted to overthrow the president. They were resisted by the elected government and by the population, who rallied on the streets in support of the democratic government. While none of this was the result of the changes initiated in the

Ministry of Education, it confirmed that those changes, aiming at opening spaces for democratic dialogue in the education system, were on a par with the kind of political future the Paraguayan people wanted for themselves.

DISCUSSION

This case portrays a different approach to the links between research and policy. The emphasis is not on research utilization but on building capacity for policy formation. Yet in this process, much more research was used—the sector assessment, the studies conducted by the research group—than had previously been the custom in Paraguay. The focus on policy dialogue as organizational learning shifted the understanding of research from an activity conducted outside the ministry to a function of management which fed naturally into consideration of alternatives for change and planning.

It should be highlighted that research-based dialogue took place in two stages, first within the Ministry of Education and then with other stakeholders for change. Dialogue was facilitated by training in management and in process and negotiation skills.

The generative effects of the intense processes of dialogue of the type illustrated in this case, which stimulated further processes of dialogue in other levels of the education system (e.g., the circles of learning among teachers), illustrates the potential of the approach for systemic change.

PART IV

Fitting It All Together

It is dangerous to synthesize the large number of complex ideas presented in this book into a few simple guidelines. Although it would have been easier to conclude this book by synthesizing the main points raised and by letting each reader draw his or her own inferences as to the practical consequences of these ideas, we have tried to do otherwise.

Knowing that at least some of our readers are most interested in informing practice, we have not resisted the temptation to try to build a model with the key elements discussed in the book. This model is not an algorithm; we do not know enough about all the relevant predictors of impact, about the nature of the independent contribution of each of them, and about the interactive effect between each predictor and the rest to be able to develop a closed model. However, we attempt to lay the foundation of a heuristic model that will indicate nine moments that critical decisions have to be made if education and policy research is to be useful for education policy reform. We want to do this from a pedagogy of raising questions, rather than from a pedagogy of providing answers, so that this framework can inform a dialogue among the agents of education research.

The framework is addressed to an agent of education research. This can be a person or an institution interested in designing and carrying out research activities which can inform policy reform. Our assumption is that ideas and knowledge are an important input to organizations and that social science research methods are a valuable resource to help organizations develop ideas and knowledge. The use of such methods requires an agent to facilitate the construction of shared knowledge. This agent could be a unit within a ministry of education or a group working under contract, such as an education department in a university, a nongovernment organization, a consulting company, or an international development agency tasked with facilitating the generation of knowledge for the purpose of informing the process of education policy formation and implementation. Of course the framework could be used by those who have to engage the services of such an agent to produce knowledge in order to inform change. The framework assumes that there is an agent, a client for the services of the agent, and a relationship between both, or a contract which specifies some systematic activities to generate knowledge that would not be available otherwise to managers and decision makers of the education system.

Chapter 13

A Model to Inform Policy with Research-Based Knowledge

The model that we propose is intended to help the agent of education research define a context-specific strategy to create knowledge for educational change. The model specifies nine situations, or moments, of action. These moments do not define a linear process of informing policy. As some moments are addressed, it will be necessary to go back to other earlier moments. The moments are presented sequentially simply because of the limitations of our capacity to express ideas. They might be visualized as arranged in circles, connected as in a coil spring, in which a moment raises questions and defines issues in the same area at different levels in the spring. A moment is never fully completed until the process of informing policy is concluded. The process of dialogue keeps bringing back questions of other moments which are answered each time from the perspective of gained experience and the perspective of the previous answers to the same question and to the related sets of questions, while we keep coming back to the same moments. Each time this is done at a higher level, depending on the information and definitions reached in the other related moments.

The nine moments of the model are as follows:

1. Define the change process to be informed by research-based knowledge
2. Define who are the stakeholders for that process of change

3. Define the current and relevant flows in the policy stream
4. Define what dialogues go on and should go on among key stakeholders
5. Empower groups for dialogue
6. Establish rules for knowledge-based dialogue
7. Design operations to generate knowledge
8. Balance technical, conceptual, and process knowledge
9. Prepare a reporting and dissemination plan

MOMENT 1: DEFINE THE CHANGE PROCESS

Who are the clients the research agent wishes to serve? Why is the agent here? At different stages of the policy formation process, it is possible that there will be varying degrees of ambiguity regarding what people want to know or the issues they care about. At what stage of the change process is the knowledge generating activity being initiated? Is knowledge being sought to discuss ongoing programs? Will the discussion be about problems for which no specific programs exist?

Research and analysis can serve several functions, such as the following:

- Inform the diagnosis of problems, answering the question, Is there a problem?
- Inform the analysis of problems, answering the question, What are the causes of the problem?
- Suggest responses to the problem, answering questions such as, Do we know what will work? and Do we know how to do it?
- Answer questions about management of programs to address the problem, such as, Is it working as expected? and How is it working?
- Answer questions about the effectiveness and efficiency of the programs, such as, Did it work? and Did the problem go away?

Though we do not adhere to a linear view of policy as proceeding in stages, it is necessary to have a sense of the timing in policy initiatives and of the timing of the key actors participating in policy formation. The research agent should establish whether the main objective for seeking knowledge is to identify problems, to suggest broad programmatic areas to address those problems, or to set up a process of continuous improvement managing specific programs and the implementation of specific policies. Other issues about the timing of key stakeholders will be important, too. Is knowledge being sought at the beginning of the time in office of a minister of education or at the end? Is knowledge being sought when an incumbent government is developing an education agenda or at the end of their tenure vis à vis a presidential election? These understandings, however poorly defined, set the initial boundaries in which the transactions of the research agent will take place.

To reach initial closure at this stage, the knowledge agent should be able to define whether the purpose of the knowledge generating activity is to solve a problem or to create a solution for an area of concern. A conceptual map should be developed showing the elements of the problem, the hypotheses people make to explain it, and the frames of reference they use in thinking about it. For example, in the study of repetition in Honduras, we developed a map (i.e., a graphic model) incorporating the information from all the interviews with key decision makers of how they explained repetition.

The knowledge agent should keep in mind that educational change will be the outcome of changes in what some people in the education system do. What people do is based on their perception of what reality is, not on reality itself. Therefore, it is necessary to understand those perceptions and to integrate new knowledge in a process which can alter those perceptions. We call this learning.

An initial understanding of what the change is about will be gained at the outset of the process. As deeper understanding is gained about the stakeholders, the possibilities for the change will be understood differently. This requires spending a lot of time talking to stakeholders, figuring out what they seek to know, what they think about the problem, and what are the issues at stake.

MOMENT 2: DEFINE THE STAKEHOLDERS

The knowledge agent should understand who has the power to influence the change process, either in policy design or implementation. Consistent with our view of policy as a series of transactions and a continuous flow between rhetoric and action, the question here is, Who are the key players for both rhetoric and action? This will include individuals, groups, and units which have formal authority or power, and those with informal power.

It is necessary to think broadly with respect to stakeholders for educational change. One of the functions dialogue can serve is to overcome the traditional isolation of many education systems. Dialogue should not be limited to educators. It should try explicitly to reach outside the education community. Many of the problems of education systems are the results of decisions made outside that system. It is these that constrain the degrees of freedom of the system to identify and implement alternatives. For instance, education budgets are the result of complex negotiations to resolve competing interests, which include the needs of other sectors, as well as the willingness of societies to be taxed and the degree to which they want to be taxed. Similarly, much legislation which influences the public sector and education is the result of processes outside the education system. Dialogue can serve to unlock these bolts by reaching out to civil society, business groups, politicians, local leaders, and others. By achieving a common vision about intermediate problems, these groups can propose and implement options within broader degrees of freedom than would be available to educators alone. The key is to get support for change at all levels; the early identification of the important actors for change is crucial.

All stakeholders of the change process should be seen as clients of the process of generating knowledge, whether they are formal clients or not. Their perceptions and actions must be influenced by the knowledge generated from research in directions supportive of change.

The knowledge agent becomes a stakeholder of the change process. The knowledge agent should work as a mediator of the dialogue informed by research activities. The knowledge agent will be a more effective mediator with the less power he or she has and the less he or she is associated with particular coalitions within the learning teams. Knowledge agents have to gain the trust of all involved in the learning process and to do this they must make themselves vulnerable to the other team members. Knowledge agents should lead the group in a process of ongoing learning but should relinquish power. The knowledge agent should not have coercive or reward power or legitimate power; that is, power stemming from position in the organization's structure. There should be no relationships of dependency between group members and the knowledge agent. The agent should be dischargeable. With time, knowledge agents will gain expert power and referent power; their influence in the group based on technical and process skills will grow, and other group members will identify with the traits or resources commanded by the knowledge agent. To the extent that an objective of developing the organization is to empower group members, the knowledge agent will seek to transfer those special skills and desirable traits to all members of the group. The agent should play the role of transformational leader, helping team members see old problems in new ways, so that research and knowledge generation become the products of all involved in the ongoing process of quality improvement.

A model should be developed to describe the stakeholders influencing the change process. This map should identify the different groups (internal and external to the education organization), their sources of power, their channels of influence, and their frequency of interaction, and whether they are for or against the type of change proposed or under consideration. The model should also specify the relations between the knowledge agent and the other stakeholders of change. This model could take an open systems view of the education system to identify key stakeholders and their transactions. An open systems view will identify the organization, the key inputs and outputs, and the internal and external environment of the organization. Internally, it will focus on goals and strategies, culture, behavior and processes, and technology and structure (Harrison, 1994).

In thinking about stakeholders and how they face a particular program or policy course, it is necessary to keep in mind that people have beliefs, motives, and intentions. Mapping out how stakeholders face a policy issue requires learning about their attitudes, motives, interests, past experience, and expectations.

MOMENT 3: DEFINE THE CURRENT AND RELEVANT FLOWS

We discuss policy formation as the outcome of the combined result of flows of policy questions or issues, policy answers, and ongoing programs. We dispute the linear model where policy follows from the identification of problems and consideration of alternatives. Instead, we see policies as evolving when a question and answer and a programmatic concern or opportunity meet. The process of generating knowledge to inform action should take account of this flow of policy concerns, answers, and programs. These define the context in which people will make sense of the knowledge generated by research.

MOMENT 4: DEFINE DIALOGUES

The process of generating knowledge for change should feed and support change teams. Some of these teams will be in existence, others will have to be created. Dialogue is seen as a tool to facilitate individual learning and the development of a shared vision for change. In the Paraguayan example, the objective was to change teaching practices at the classroom level. This required dialogue between teachers and between teachers and principals at the school level. Also, dialogue had to take place between supervisors, between supervisors and principals, between senior staff in the Ministry of Education, and between the members of the team in charge of organizing the training programs. This defines four loops of dialogue at different levels, all of which must be linked with each other. Knowledge about the alternative approaches to train teachers and about the results of ongoing efforts should be entered into the dialogue in these four loops.

The result of this activity should be a proposal for frequent communication among key stakeholders for change. In thinking about the stakeholder groups, it is necessary to define if dialogue will be more productive if it takes place in homogeneous or cross-functional teams. For purposes of problem identification, a wide range of different homogeneous teams where people from the same level and background meet will be better. For purposes of exploration of alternatives, cross-functional teams where people from different backgrounds, sectors, and levels interact will be better.

The proposal should specify the prerequisites to get people in the groups to talk freely and openly and the ways to ground this discussion in research-based knowledge.

MOMENT 5: EMPOWER GROUPS

Dialogue does not happen automatically when people are brought together. In fact, because there are so many barriers to effective communication in organizations, most people brought together will have a history that will impede rather than facilitate dialogue. If research-based knowledge is to feed organizational dialogue, the conditions will have to be created to facilitate such dialogue. This involves investing in helping people to talk to each other in groups, facilitating the development of trust among group members, and helping participants to learn how to use and construct knowledge in their dialogues. It means making efforts to convert groups of people into teams of change.

In the early stages of group formation, professional facilitators can conduct team-building exercises to help group members work more effectively with each other. Individual team members need to learn to communicate openly and honestly, to confront differences and resolve conflicts, and to sublimate personal goals for the good of the team. This is a major goal of organization development in education systems. Efforts to bring knowledge to inform policy formation must work in tandem with efforts to develop organizations in this way.

Establishing conditions for dialogue should take notice of the larger conditions and environment where the change team operates. Is this a context which is highly authoritarian? Is there much tradition of participatory dialogue? Can team members trust each other? A central condition for dialogue is trust—between team members and between them and the knowledge agent. The development of trust is paramount to sustained ongoing processes of improvement based on dialogue.

In specific contexts, process facilitators will have to determine the best ways to help groups reach decisions and produce effectively. Most groups use face-to-face interaction, the most common and easiest way of group interaction. Other alternatives include: brainstorming, the nominal group technique—group participants are asked to produce solutions individually after group exchange and prior to further exchange; Delphi exercises, to obtain consensus among group members; ideawriting, a method for developing ideas and exploring their meaning; and interpretive structural modeling, a method to identify relationships among the key aspects which define an issue or problem (Moore, 1994). The goal of team discussions should not necessarily be to reach consensus on a uniform view of problems and alternatives. This would prove very difficult in groups with diverse views and values. Instead, the goal should be to build coalitions and negotiate basic understandings so that all key stakeholders can support a change program even if they do it for different reasons or with reference to different value systems and goals.

How can the knowledge agent gain trust? Trust is earned by demonstrating openness and integrity, by frequently sharing knowledge in an honest and truthful way, by demonstrating technical competence, and by showing consistency, dependability, and loyalty to the members of the team. The knowledge agent must be willing to make himself or herself vulnerable to other members of the team, to help them save face and protect them, and to demonstrate a capacity to put the gains of the team above his or her own personal gains.

One way knowledge agents can gain trust is by understanding the difference between sponsors and clients of the activity. Team participants should believe that he who is paying the player is not necessarily calling the tune and that there is freedom to explore ideas and to generate alternatives outside the preferred options of the formal authorities or of the sponsors of the activity.

A key aspect of facilitating group development will be to discern when the group should go public with deliberations and when it should not. The kind of large-scale change we discuss in the book and illustrate in the cases eventually requires discussions with large numbers of stakeholders so that all can support reform at all levels. But it is not practical to initiate discussions about reforms simultaneously at all levels of the system. Change starts with dialogue at some entry points in the system, with smaller discussions in some change teams. The question of how long these groups should discuss before they reach out to other groups is critical. If they spend too little time, the ideas offered to stimulate larger dialogue will be insufficiently developed, the understandings reached by the group about needs or problems will be incomplete, and there will be risks that pressures stemming from discussions with other groups will exacerbate internal conflicts in the initial change group.

Groups will go through different stages. Initially there may be ambiguity and skepticism about the function and sustainability of the group. Later on, conflicts will emerge, a sign that the group is serving its purpose of making conflict overt. The commitment of participants to the process may weaken. Some managers or individuals will resist the power the group has gained on their autonomy through shared information. Facilitators of the dialogue should watch for signs of commitment for participation, should observe who is meeting schedules and deadlines, should note whether the agreed-to products are being produced, and should keep track of who is showing up at meetings. It is only after these stages have been resolved that team participants will reach a peak in performance and productivity. Process facilitation should attend to the stages of group formation and performance and help team participants reach stages of peak performance and overcome conflict and resistance stages. Change teams should go public; that is, engage other groups in the process of dialogue after reaching a stage of peak productivity, and after solving the initial stages of skepticism, ambiguity, and internal conflict. Of course, change groups can see dialogue as a mechanism of continuous improvement of processes.

Dialogue within the early change teams should not stop once they go public. In fact, after a round of discussions with other groups the initial change team can go back to dialogue informed by feedback and other perspectives. This is illustrated in the preparation of the strategic education plan in Paraguay. The strategic dialogue group (initial change team) spent several months in dialogue about the needs and main problems of the education system and about the options for change. As a result of the period of peak performance, they produced a proposal for dialogue, a synthesis of the 2,000 pages of analysis and options for change they had discussed. They engaged multiple groups of stakeholders in more than twenty roundtables. At the end of this second stage of dialogue, the strategic dialogue group reconvened and prepared a strategic plan using the feedback received in the second stage of dialogue.

Achieving effective dialogue in change teams requires spending time on process. This involves teaching team participants how to listen to each other, training in negotiations and conflict resolution, developing rules for dialogue at the outset, and monitoring compliance with rules. Process management will require substantial investments once the group is formed and periodic checking and intervention throughout the life of the team.

MOMENT 6: ESTABLISH RULES

Dialogue is not consultation. It is a means to develop knowledge out of research and the confrontation of values and priorities among team participants integrating their personal knowledge derived from experience and other sources. Dialogue is not the blind acceptance of the expert power of researchers by team participants. The achievement of a balanced discussion of knowledge generated by research in a change team is a delicate challenge. A facilitator of dialogue sessions should be appointed to maintain focus and prevent the discussion from being sidetracked.

The importance of basic rules of dialogue should not be underestimated. It will be important to nominate a convener for the group, organize a process to develop an agenda for group meetings, distribute the agenda and materials in advance, and agree on time and length of meetings. A group facilitator should keep discussions focused, encourage participation by all, encourage the expression of conflict and resolution, and encourage the clash of ideas focusing on issues and not on personalities.

Construction of common knowledge in these change teams should benefit from processes which encourage creativity and which do not limit the contributions of individual participants. As part of the process, facilitation groups should learn to spend moments in which problems are examined and alternatives are generated without criticism.

Contrary to what would appear commonsensical, we have learned that teams advance further and in less time if they do not start with discussions of broad outcomes or goals but concentrate on intermediate objectives or problems. In our experience, disagreement is more likely if dialogue starts either with broad societal goals or with very specific strategies and programs for improvement. Broad goals refer to value systems and ideologies and it may not be practical, or reasonable, to expect people to agree on those. Similarly, without a common vision of what the general problems and priority areas are, discussion of specific strategies and actions will be long. Because the goal of dialogue should not be to achieve consensus but to build coalitions around a change program, there is no reason to focus on the value systems or goals in order for people to decide the important actions. In practical terms, people of different religious or political beliefs can agree on the main problems of the education system. They do not need to all join a common faith or political doctrine to build a coalition to address education problems. For instance, rather than hoping to achieve an agreement on the new vision of society, a group can find common ground quickly if they concentrate on intermediate problems of the outcomes of education systems, such as: How much do students learn? Who learns and who does not? and Why? Once a common vision is achieved around these intermediate problems or objectives, discussion about specific strategies to address these problems will be easier.

In order for the participatory dialogue we have outlined here to contribute to decision making, there must be an adequate time to participate. Issues in which members of change teams participate must be relevant to their interests. They must have the ability to participate (i.e., the intelligence, technical knowledge, and communication skills) and the larger organizational context must be supportive of participation.

MOMENT 7: DESIGN OPERATIONS
TO GENERATE KNOWLEDGE

In furthering dialogue for organizational learning, research-based knowledge will not always be desirable or feasible. For this reason, one of the moments focuses explicitly on determining whether research-based knowledge makes sense and which kind of research-based knowledge makes the most sense.

Organizations and managers do not have the time to develop or consume the best possible knowledge in order to inform an issue or policy. Given scarcity of time and resources, they must satisfy rather than optimize or maximize. The agent in charge of facilitating the development of knowledge must ask what type of knowledge will do. The questions raised in Chapter 2 with respect to mapping the policy dialogue space will help to develop knowledge that satisfies the following questions: (1) Is the problem to be addressed convergent or divergent? (2) What tools and disciplines are sufficient to solve the problem? and (3) Can the problem be solved by technical knowledge?

We know that in situations where a high level of uncertainty exists, when there is little precedence to draw on, when variables are less scientifically predictable, where facts are limited or do not clearly point the way to go, when analytical data are of little use, and when there are several plausible alternatives, most senior managers will use intuitive decision making. In this case, dialogue may be a way to make the implicit maps which inform such intuitive decision making explicit and to design research which can inform core assumptions of those maps.

In other cases, it will make sense to inform dialogue with research of some kind. It is imperative that research design takes into account what people want to know and when they want to know it, and that it addresses areas about which they can do something.

All the methods discussed in Chapter 5—survey research, consultations, sector assessments, evaluations, generating data from information systems, and preparing policy briefs—may be appropriate at this stage. While the research methodologies will be those used by social scientists, the approach and the context in which they are used will be different. Research should begin with the client in mind, possibly developed jointly with the client.

What is critical is that this research will be embedded in a process of consulting. Frequent communication and reporting will change the reality that research is trying to capture and understand. This is all right. The assumptions of research in the physical sciences do not hold here. The research necessary to inform action and change in human organizations will only be possible if people cooperate by providing truthful information. There is no reason to expect they will do this if there will not be positive consequences for them from cooperating.

MOMENT 8: BALANCE TECHNICAL, CONCEPTUAL, AND PROCESS KNOWLEDGE

Effective dialogue about research-based dialogue will take good technical analysis and research. Dialogue can result in good conceptual maps about the context where research is taking place (i.e., maps about the problem to be addressed, about stakeholders for change, or about the context where research and knowledge are being used). It would be inappropriate to spend all your energies developing sound technical knowledge and end up having little knowledge about the organizational context where that knowledge is going to be used. Similarly, knowledge about the process of interaction among the participants in the change teams is essential to keep this process moving and to help the team reach deeper stages of dialogue and learning.

Achieving this balance takes technical skills, process skills (i.e., the ability to work with, understand, and motivate other people; the ability to listen and understand the needs of others; and the ability to manage conflict), and conceptual skills (i.e., the conceptualization of maps of complex situations, the analysis and diagnosis of complex situations, spotting problems, identifying alternatives that can correct them, evaluating the alternatives, and selecting alternatives).

MOMENT 9: PREPARE A REPORTING PLAN

While our emphasis regarding the role of ideas to promote organizational change in education systems is on the process to develop
those ideas and knowledge, there are some tangible products or
mechanisms which are used for the exchange, reporting, and dissemination of this knowledge. These products can be summaries of
agreements of group meetings, declarations to the press, preliminary or final reports, briefs to other groups, or communications of
decisions made or actions in progress. The exchange of those products should not be an afterthought of the dialogue process; they
should be anticipated at the stage of identifying stakeholders and
the kind of dialogue which needs to take place. There may be significant financial and technical requirements for effective communication to certain groups.

The first question in preparing a reporting plan is to map the system of dialogues which will take place among different groups of
stakeholders. Reports from the dialogue of some groups will be inputs to the dialogue or action of other groups. For instance, the
strategic dialogue group in Paraguay decided to launch a massive
public communication campaign to parents and teachers to promote participation at the school level and to encourage dialogue at
that level. Similarly, that group prepared a proposal for dialogue
for the roundtables of social, political, and business leaders that
provided input for the preparation of the strategic plan. This required preparing a document and printing thousands of copies, preparing a set of graphic presentations, and preparing a videotape to
allow the group facilitators to summarize the early discussions of
the strategic dialogue group. To motivate further discussion about
the plan, a series of meetings with key owners of newspapers, television, and radio stations allowed wide press coverage of the basic
proposals contained in the plan for discussion and outlined the
process to be followed and the mechanisms to provide feedback.
After the roundtables in which the proposal was discussed took
place, a final document was prepared. This was the strategic education plan. Again, thousands of copies of this were made and distributed. A series of press interviews of key officials of the dialogue
group, and detailed press coverage of the basic proposals contained
in the plan, allowed dissemination of these ideas to the public.

In developing the model of dialogue that should take place to
initiate and sustain change, the important questions to keep in mind
are, Who needs to know what and when? and What is the best way
to get the information to them that will develop that knowledge?
Long, written reports are not the most effective mechanism to reach

wide audiences. Executive briefs or short conversations work best with senior decision makers. Facilitators or discussion guides for workshops or discussion sessions work best to convey information to groups of teachers or supervisors. The advantage to circulating drafts of reports to request feedback is that they get more timely attention than final reports.

As we are not advocating a diffusion and dissemination approach of research results as an effective mechanism to support policy reform, the diffusion of ideas and the reporting plan to do this should not be understood as the ultimate aspect of the process. As we argue throughout the book, dialogue where stakeholders can integrate these ideas with their knowledge and experience will be most effective in helping them learn and construct new knowledge. However, dissemination of ideas is still necessary to permit this dialogue. Key questions about the reporting plan are whether the information disseminated is relevant to real problems, whether it addresses the practical concerns of those who receive it, whether they can understand it and trust it, and whether they receive it in time to discuss it and use it.

Given our emphasis on organizational learning at all levels of the education system—inside and outside education—a key aspect of the dissemination plan is to develop capacity for informed policy debate and advocacy at all levels. This refers back to the notion of empowering groups for dialogue.

Just as it made sense to think broadly about stakeholders for educational change, it makes sense here to think broadly with respect to disseminating information that can inform dialogue. It is important to spread technical knowledge as widely as possible, using multiple media and channels. Toro (1992) has developed a model of social mobilization in education based on the notion of a reeditor. The basic notion in this model is that people receive information from other persons whom they trust. Reeditors are persons who have the trust of a specific group. Reeditors can be empowered by providing them with training and information (in the form of posters or leaflets) which they can distribute to others. Their message can be strengthened with spots on the radio or television.

CONCLUSION

In one of his lyrics, John Lennon said, "Life is what happens to you while you are busy making other plans." Educational change, like life, often happens while researchers and policy makers are busy making other plans. The change that matters, of course, is the one that takes place in schools and classrooms, not the one intended in research reports or plan documents. A changed education system is one where people do things differently and where they can talk about what they are doing differently, why they are doing it, and with what results. Only when many conversations about change construct a vision and an enabling environment for it in the public sphere can conditions in schools begin to improve. While we do not think that education researchers can, or should, define the direction of educational change, they can organize their practice in ways that can be most helpful for organizational learning and change by explicitly thinking about the nine moments we have suggested here. This requires recognizing the limitations of their own expertise to define which way education systems should go, and to see themselves as stakeholders in a dynamic process of dialogue with others whose interactions define what education systems do and fail to do.

By recognizing that education systems are not machines but are arenas for conflict, and that what education systems do reflects how people construct their roles regarding those systems, researchers can facilitate the development of knowledge and sustained organizational learning. The key guides are democratic dialogue, empowerment, time, persistence, and patience. This model is not a panacea, a quick fix, or a magic bullet that will lead to success everywhere. But we have learned to prefer it to the alternatives.

References

Ackoff, R. 1974. *Redesigning the future*. New York: John Wiley.

Agarwala, R. 1983. *Planning in developing countries*. Washington, D.C.: World Bank Staff Working Papers.

Aguerrondo, I. 1996. *La escuela como organizacion inteligente*. Buenos Aires: Troquel.

Alkhafaji, A. F. 1989. *A stakeholder approach to corporate governance: Managing in a dynamic environment*. New York: Quorum Books.

Allison, G. T. 1971. *Essence of decision: Explaining the Cuban missile crisis*. Boston: Little, Brown.

Ansoff, I. 1965. *Corporate Strategy*. New York: McGraw-Hill.

Appadurai, A. 1990. Disjuncture and difference in the global cultural economy. In *Global culture*, ed. M. Featherstone, 295–310. London: Sage.

Argyris, C., and D. A. Schon. 1978. *Organizational learning: A theory of action perspective*. Reading, Mass.: Addison-Wesley.

Ayers, T. D. 1987. Stakeholders as partners in evaluation: A stakeholder-collaborative approach. *Evaluation and Program Planning* 10(3): 263–271.

Bamberger, M. 1991. The politics of evaluation in developing countries. *Evaluation and Program Planning* 14(4): 325–339.

Bell, C. L. G. 1974. The political framework. In *Redistribution with growth*, ed. H. Chenery et al. New York: Oxford University Press.

Benveniste, G. 1991. *Mastering the politics of planning*. San Francisco: Jossey-Bass.

Bohme, G., and N. Stehr, eds. 1986. *The knowledge society: The growing impact of scientific knowledge on social relations*. Norwell, Mass.: Kluwer.

Brandon, P. R., M. A. Lindberg, and Z. Wang. 1993a. Enhancing validity through beneficiaries' equitable involvement in evaluation. *Evaluation and Program Planning* 16(4): 287–293.

Brandon, P. R., M. A. Lindberg, and Z. Wang. 1993b. Involving program beneficiaries in the early stages of evaluation: Issues of consequential validity and influence. *Educational Evaluation and Policy Analysis* 15(4): 420–428.

Braverman, H. 1974. *Labor and monopoly capital.* New York: Monthly Review Press.

Braybrooke, D., and C. E. Lindblom. 1963. *A strategy of decision: Policy evaluation as a social process.* New York: Free Press.

Bryk, A. S., ed. 1983. *Stakeholder-based evaluation.* San Francisco: Jossey-Bass.

Bryson, J. 1990. *Strategic planning for public and nonprofit organizations.* San Francisco: Jossey-Bass.

Buchert, L., and K. King, eds. 1996. *Consultancy and research in international education.* Bonn: German Foundation for International Development.

Caplan, N. S., and others. 1975. *The use of social science knowledge in policy decisions at the national level.* Ann Arbor: Institute for Social Research, University of Michigan.

Cariola, P. 1996. Lessons learned from REDUC (1972–1992). In *Crossing lines: Research and policy networks for developing country education,* ed. N. F. McGinn, 155–157. Westport, Conn.: Praeger.

Carton, M. 1996. Educational networking in French-speaking West Africa: Hope or fallacy? In *Crossing lines: Research and policy networks for developing country education,* ed. N. F. McGinn, 113–116. Westport, Conn.: Praeger.

Cassidy, T. 1996. A framework for organizing information system interventions. Paper presented at Annual Conference of the Comparative and International Education Society, March, Williamsburg, Virginia.

Chapman, D., and C. Carrier, eds. 1990. *Improving educational quality: A global perspective.* New York: Greenwood Press.

Chapman, D., and L. Mahlck. 1993. *From data to action: Information systems in educational planning.* Paris: International Institute for Educational Planning, UNESCO.

Clune, W. 1993. The best path to systemic educational policy: Standard/decentralized or differentiated/decentralized? *Educational Evaluation and Policy Analysis* 15(3): 233–254.

Coleman, J. 1966. *Equality of educational opportunity.* Washington, D.C.: U.S. Department of Health, Education, and Welfare, Office of Education.

Collins, D. 1989. Organizational harm, legal condemnation and stakeholder retaliation: A typology, research agenda and application. *Journal of Business Ethics* 8(1): 1–13.

Cousins, J. B., and L. M. Earl. 1992. The case for participatory evaluation. *Educational Evaluation and Policy Analysis* 14(4): 397–418.

Crouch, L. A. 1993. Success in policy reform through policy dialogue. Research Triangle Park, N.C.: Research Triangle Institute, unpublished working paper.

Crouch, L. A., E. Vegas, and R. Johnson. 1993. *Policy dialogue and reform in the education sector: Necessary steps and conditions.* Research Triangle Park, N.C.: Research Triangle Institute, Center for International Development.

Darling-Hammond, L., and M. W. McLaughlin. 1995. Policies that support professional development in an era of reform. *Phi Delta Kappan* 76(8): 597–604.

Davies, L. 1990. *Equity and efficiency? School management in an international context.* London: Falmer Press.

Davis, R. G. 1986. Trip report on Egypt in a memorandum prepared on October 16, 1986. Cambridge, Mass.: Harvard Institute for International Development.

DeLeon, P. 1992. The democratization of the policy science. *Public Administration Review* 52(2): 125–129.

Derthick, M. 1972. *New towns in-town: Why a federal program failed.* Washington, D.C.: Urban Institute.

Deutsch, K. 1966. *Nationalism and social communication.* New York: MIT Press.

Donors to African Education Task Force. 1993. Who owns the programmes? Issue raised during dialogue on African education. In *IIEP Newsletter,* January–March 1994.

Doron, G. 1986. Telling the big stories—Policy responses to analytical complexity: A comment. *Journal of Policy Analysis and Management* 5(4): 798–802.

Downs, G. W., and P. D. Larkey. 1986. *The search for government efficiency: From hubris to helplessness.* Philadelphia: Temple University Press.

Drucker, P. F. 1993. *Post–capitalist society.* Oxford: Butterworth-Heinemann.

Dunn, W. N. 1980. The two-communities metaphorical model of knowledge use: An exploratory case study. *Knowledge: Creation, Diffusion, Culture* 1(4): 515–537.

Elley, W. 1992. *How in the world do students read? IEA study of reading literacy.* Newark, Del.: International Reading Association, International Association for the Evaluation of Educational Achievement.

Feldman, C. 1989. *Order without design: Information production and policy making.* Stanford, Calif.: Stanford University Press.

FLACSO. 1995. *Es posible concertar las politicas educativas?* Buenos Aires: Mino y Davila Editores.

Flores, F. 1995. *Creando organizaciones para el futuro.* Santiago, Chile: Dolmen Ediciones.

Forester, J. 1989. *Planning in the face of power.* Berkeley: University of California Press.

Freeman, R. E. 1984. *Strategic management: A stakeholder approach.* Boston: Pitman.

Friedmann, J. 1987. *Planning in the public domain: From knowledge to action.* Princeton, N.J.: Princeton University Press.

Fuhrman, S., and S. M. Johnson. 1994. Lessons from Victoria. *Phi Delta Kappan* 75(10): 770–772, 774.

Fuller, B. 1987. What school factors raise student achievement in the Third World? *Review of Educational Research* 57(2): 255–292.

Fuller, B., and P. Clarke. 1994. Raising school effects while ignoring culture? Local conditions and the influence of classroom tools, rules and pedagogy. *Review of Educational Research* 64(1): 119–157.

Gellner, E. 1983. *Nations and nationalism.* Westport, Conn.: Westwood.

Gibbons, M., C. Limojes, H. Nowatney, S. Schwartzmann, P. Scott, and M. Trow. 1995. *The new production of knowledge: The dynamics of science and research in contemporary societies.* London: Sage.

Godet, M. 1991. *From anticipation to action: A handbook of strategic prospective.* Paris: UNESCO.

Grindle, M. S. 1980. *Politics and policy implementation in the Third World.* Princeton, N.J.: Princeton University Press.

Habermas, J. 1971. *Knowledge and human interests.* Boston: Beacon Press.

Hallett, M. A., and R. Rogers. 1994. The push for "Truth in sentencing": Evaluating competing stakeholders. *Evaluation and Program Planning* 17(2): 187–196.

Hannaway, J., and M. Carnoy. 1993. *Decentralization and school improvement: Can we fulfill the promise?* San Francisco: Jossey-Bass.

Harrison, M. 1994. *Diagnosing organizations.* Thousand Oaks, Calif.: Sage.

Hatten, K., and M. L. Hatten. 1988. *Effective strategic management analysis and action.* Englewood Cliffs, N.J.: Prentice-Hall.

Havelock, R. G. 1972. *Bibliography on knowledge utilization and dissemination.* Ann Arbor: Center for Research on the Utilization of Scientific Knowledge, University of Michigan.

Henry, G. T., K. C. Dickey, and J. C. Areson. 1991. Stakeholder participation in educational performance monitoring systems. *Educational Evaluation and Policy Analysis* 13(2): 177–188.

Herman, J., L. Lyons-Morris, and C. T. Fitz-Gibbon. 1987. *Evaluator's handbook.* Newbury Park, Calif.: Sage.

Heyneman, S. P. 1995. Economics of education: Disappointments and potential. *Prospects* 25(4): 559–583.

Hoos, I. R. 1971. *Systems analysis in public policy: A critique.* Berkeley: University of California Press.

Hopkins, D., ed. 1989. *Improving the quality of schooling: Lessons from the OECD International School Improvement project.* London: Falmer Press.

Husen, T. 1984. Issues and their background. In *Educational research and policy. How do they relate?* ed. T. Husen and M. Kogan. Oxford: Pergamon Press.

Husen, T. 1994. Educational research and policy-making. In *International encyclopedia of education,* ed. T. Husen and N. Postlethwaite, 1857–1864. Oxford: Pergamon Press.

Husen, T., and M. Kogan, eds. 1984. *Educational research and policy. How do they relate?* Oxford: Pergamon Press.

Improving the Efficiency of Education Systems (IEES). 1986. *Indonesia. Education and human resources sector review.* Tallahassee: Learning Systems Institute, Florida State University.

IEES. 1988a. *Liberia. Education and human resources sector assessment.* Tallahassee: Learning Systems Institute, Florida State University.

IEES. 1988b. *Nepal. Education and human resources sector assessment.* Tallahassee: Learning Systems Institute, Florida State University.

Kannapel, P. J., B. D. Moore, P. Coe, and L. Aagaard. 1995. Six heads are better than one? School-based decision making in rural Kentucky. *Journal of Research in Rural Education* 11(1): 15–23.

Kanter, R. M. 1990. *When giants learn to dance.* New York: Touchstone Books.

Kelly, M., and S. Maynard-Moody. 1993. Policy analysis in the post–positivist era: Engaging stakeholders in evaluating the economic development districts program. *Public Administration Review* 53(2): 135–142.

Kemmerer, F. 1994. *Utilizing education and human resource sector analyses.* Paris: International Institute for Educational Planning, UNESCO.

King, K. 1996. Networking as a knowledge system. In *Crossing lines: Research and policy networks for developing country education,* ed. N. F. McGinn, 19–21. Westport, Conn.: Praeger.

Kogan, M., N. Konnan, and M. Henkel. 1980. *Government's commissioning of research: A case study.* Uxbridge, England: Department of Government, Brunel University.

Lampinen, O. 1992. *The utilization of social science research in public policy.* Helsinki: Vapk-Publishing, Government Printing Centre.

Langtry, B. 1994. Stakeholders and the moral responsibilities of business. *Business Ethics Quarterly* 4(4): 445–458.

Lauglo, J. 1995. Forms of decentralization and their implications for evaluation. *Comparative Education* 31(1): 5–29.

Lawler, E., A. Mohrman, S. Mohrman, G. Ledford, T. Cummings, and Associates. 1985. *Doing research that is useful for theory and practice.* San Francisco: Jossey-Bass.

Lawrence, J. E. S. 1989. Engaging recipients in development evaluation: The stakeholder approach. *Evaluation Review* 13(3): 243–256.

Levin, H. 1982. Why isn't educational research more useful? *Prospects* 8(2): 157–166.

Linstone, H. A., and A. J. Meltsner. 1984. *Multiple perspectives for decision making: Bridging the gap between analysis and action.* New York: North-Holland, Elsevier Science Publishing.

Lockheed, M., and A. Verspoor. 1991. *Improving primary education in developing countries: A review of policy options.* Washington, D.C.: World Bank.

Loera, A. 1988. The Third World educational research database. Cambridge, Mass.: Harvard Institute for International Development, BRIDGES project. Unpublished paper.

Lynn, L. E., Jr. 1989. Policy analysis in the bureaucracy: How new? How effective? *Journal of Policy Analysis and Management* 8(3): 373–377.

Malen, B., R. Ogawa, and J. Kranz. 1990. What do we know about school-based management? A case study of the literature. In *Choice and control in American education.* Vol. 2, *The practice of choice, decentralization and school restructuring,* ed. W. Clune and J. Witte. London: Falmer Press.

March, J. G., and H. A. Simon. 1958. *Organizations.* New York: Wiley and Sons.

Marjoe, G., and A. Wildavsky. 1979. Implementation as evolution. In *Implementation*, 3rd ed., ed. J. Pressman and A. Wildavsky, 163–180. Berkeley and Los Angeles: University of California Press.

Maxwell, J. A., and Y. S. Lincoln. 1990. Methodology and epistemology: A dialogue. *Harvard Educational Review* 60(9): 497–512.

Mayer, O. G. 1990. Policy dialogue between multilateral institutions and developing countries. *Intereconomic: Review of Trade and Development* 25: 163–170.

McGinn, N. 1994. The impact of supranational organizations on public education. *International Journal of Educational Development* 14(3): 289–298.

McGinn, N., and A. Borden. 1995. *Framing questions, constructing answers: Linking research with education policy for developing countries.* Cambridge, Mass.: Harvard Institute for International Development and Harvard University Press.

McGinn, N., and S. Street. 1986. Educational decentralization: Weak state or strong state? *Comparative Education Review* 30(4): 471–490.

McGinn, N. F., ed. 1996. *Crossing lines: Research and policy networks for developing country education.* Westport, Conn.: Praeger.

McKillip, H. 1987. *Need analysis.* Thousand Oaks, Calif.: Sage.

Mingat, A., and J.-P. Tang. 1988. *Analytical tools for sector work in education.* Washington, D.C. World Bank.

Moore, C. 1994. *Group techniques for idea building.* Thousand Oaks, Calif.: Sage.

Nunez-Collado, A. 1994. *Concertacion: La cultura del dialogo.* Republica Dominicana: Pontificia Universidad Madre y Maestra.

Ojeda Delgado, A. 1994. Educación superior, economia y sociedad en el occidente de México. *Comercio Exterior* 44(3): 253–257.

Oman, C. 1994. *Globalisation and regionalisation: The challenge for developing countries.* Paris: Organization of Economic Cooperation and Development (OECD).

Pigozzi, M. J., and V. Cieutat. 1988. *Education and human resources sector assessment manual.* Tallahassee: Florida State University.

Porter, R. 1995. *Knowledge utilization and the process of policy formation. Toward a framework for Africa.* Washington, D.C.: Academy for Educational Development.

Postlethwaite, T. N. 1994. Research and policy-making in education: Some possible links. In *Educational research and policy. How do they relate?* ed. T. Husen and M. Kogan. Oxford: Pergamon Press.

Prawda, J. 1992. *Educational decentralization in Latin America: Lessons learned.* Washington, D.C.: World Bank, A View from LATHR No. 27.

Pressman, J. L., and A. B. Wildavsky. 1979. *Implementation: How great expectations in Washington are dashed in Oakland.* Berkeley: University of California Press.

Psacharopoulos, G. 1986. The planning of education: Where do we stand? *Comparative Education Review* 30(4): 560–573.

Psacharopoulos, G. 1990. Comparative education: From theory to practice, or are you A;\neo.* or B;*.ist? *Comparative Education Review* 34(3): 369–380.

Psacharopoulos, G., and M. Woodhall. 1985. *Education for development: An analysis of investment choices.* New York: Oxford University Press.

Reich, M. R., and D. M. Cooper. 1995. *Political mapping: Computer-assisted political analysis.* Newton Center, Mass.: PoliMap.

Reich, R. B., ed. 1988. *The power of public ideas.* Cambridge, Mass.: Ballinger.

Reimers, F. 1997a. Participation, policy dialogue and education sector analysis. In *Education and development. Tradition and innovation.* Vol. 1, *Concepts, approaches and assumptions,* ed. J. Lynch, C. Modgil, and S. Modgil. London: Cassell.

Reimers, F. 1997b. The role of the community in expanding educational opportunities. The EDUCO schools in El Salvador. In *Education and development. Tradition and innovation.* Vol. 2, *Equity and excellence in education for development,* ed. J. Lynch, C. Modgil, and S. Modgil. London: Cassell.

Reimers, F., ed. 1995. *La educacion en El Salvador de cara al siglo XXI: Desafios y oportunidades.* San Salvador: UCA Editores.

Reimers, F., N. McGinn, and K. Wild. 1995. *Confronting future challenges: Educational information, research and decision-making.* Paris: International Bureau of Education, UNESCO.

Rhenman, E. 1968. *Industrial democracy and industrial management.* London: Tavistock Institute.

Richardson, A., C. Jackson, and W. Sykes. 1990. *Taking research seriously.* London: Department of Health.

Rondinelli, D., J. Middleton, and A. M. Verspoor. 1990. *Planning education reform in developing countries: The contingency approach.* Durham: University of North Carolina Press.

Salmen, L. F. 1989. Beneficiary assessment: Improving the design and implementation of development projects. *Evaluation Review* 13(3): 273–291.

Sander, B. 1996. *Gestion educativa en America Latina.* Buenos Aires: Troquel.

Schlossberger, E. 1994. A new model of business: Dual-Invester theory. *Business Ethics Quarterly* 4(4): 459–474.

Schumacher, E. F. 1977. *A guide for the perplexed.* New York: Harper and Row.

Senge, P. M. 1990. *The fifth discipline: The art and practice of the learning organization.* New York: Doubleday.

Shaeffer, S., and J. A. Nkinyangi, eds. 1983. *Educational research environments in the development world.* Ottawa: International Development Research Centre.

Shavelson, R. 1988. Contributions of educational research to policy and practice: Constructing, challenging, changing cognition. *Educational Researcher* 17(7): 4–11.

Shulman, L. 1990. *Research in teaching and learning.* New York: Macmillan.

Simon, H. A. 1969. *The sciences of the artificial.* Cambridge, Mass.: MIT Press.

Snow, C. P. 1959. *The two cultures and the scientific revolution.* New York: Cambridge University Press.

Snyder, C. W., ed. 1991. *Consultation of change. Proceedings of the Etosha conference.* Tallahassee: Learning Systems Institute, Florida State University.

Snyder, W. 1994. Personal telephone communication, 26 May.

Stake, R., ed. 1975. *Evaluating the art in education: A responsive approach.* Columbus, Ohio: Merrill.

Stokey, E., and R. Zeckhauser. 1978. *A primer for policy analysis.* New York: W. W. Norton.

Stoner, J. A. F., and R. E. Freeman. 1992. *Management.* Englewood Cliffs, N.J.: Prentice-Hall.

Tatto, M., D. Nielsen, and W. Cummings. 1991. *Comparing the effects and costs of different approaches for educating primary school teachers: The case of Sri Lanka.* Cambridge, Mass.: Harvard University.

Thompson, R. J. 1991. Facilitating commitment, consensus, credibility, and visibility through collaborative foreign assistance project evaluations. *Evaluation and Program Planning* 14(4): 341–350.

Timar, T. B., and D. L. Kirp. 1989. Education reform in the 1980s: Lessons from the States. *Phi Delta Kappan* 70(7): 504–511.

Toffler, A. 1990. *Powershift: Knowledge, wealth and violence at the edge of the 21st century.* New York: Bantam.

Toro, B. 1992. La calidad de la educacion primaria, medios de comunicacion masiva y comunidad civil. *Boletin del Proyecto Principal de Educacion para America Latina y Caribe* 28: 91–120.

Trow, M. 1994. Policy analysis. In *International encyclopedia of education,* ed. T. Husen and N. Postlethwaite, 4550–4556. Oxford: Pergamon Press.

United States Agency for International Development (USAID). 1990. *Lessons learned in basic education in the developing world.* Washington, D.C.: Bureau for Science and Technology, Office of Education.

Velez, E., E. Schiefelbein, and J. Valenzuela. 1993. *Factors affecting achievement in primary education.* Washington, D.C.: World Bank.

Vielle, J. P. 1981. *The impact of research on educational change.* Ottawa: International Development Research Centre.

Villegas-Reimers, E. 1994. La reforma educativa venezolana de 1980: Una evaluacion de su impacto en la educacion de maestros en relacion a los nuevos programas de educacion basica. *Revista Paraguaya de Sociologia* 89: 225–234.

Villegas-Reimers, E. 1996. Values in education in the primary and secondary school curriculum: A cross-country study in Latin America and the Caribbean. In *Education and development. Tradition and innovation.* Vol. 3, *Innovations in delivering primary education,* ed. J. Lynch, C. Modgil, and S. Modgil. London: Cassell.

Villegas-Reimers, E., and F. Reimers. 1996. Where are 60 million teachers? The missing voice in educational reforms around the world. *Prospects* 26(3): 469–492.

Walberg, H. J., and R. P. Niemiec. 1994. Is Chicago school reform working? *Phi Delta Kappan* 75(9): 713–715.

Warwick, D. P. 1982. *Bitter pills.* Cambridge: Cambridge University Press.

Warwick, D. P., and F. Reimers. 1995. *Hope or despair?* Westport, Conn.: Praeger.

Warwick, D. P., F. Reimers, and N. McGinn. 1992. The implementation of educational innovations: Lessons from Pakistan. *International Journal of Educational Development* 12(1): 297–307.

Webber, D. J. 1991. The distribution and use of policy knowledge in the policy process. *Knowledge and Policy* 4(4): 6–35.

Weiss, C. H. 1979. The many meanings of research utilization. *Public Administration Review* (Sept.–Oct.): 426–431.

Weiss, C. H. 1983. The stakeholder approach to evaluation: Origins and promise. In *Stakeholder-based evaluation new,* ed. A. S. Bryk. San Francisco: Jossey-Bass.

Weiss, C. H. 1989. Congressional committees as users of analysis. *Journal of Policy Analysis and Management* 8(3): 411–431.

Weiss, C. H., ed. 1977. *Using social science research in public policy making.* Lexington, Mass.: Lexington Books.

Weiss, J. W. 1994. *Business ethics: A managerial, stakeholder approach.* Belmont, Calif.: Wadsworth Publishing.

Welsh, T. 1993. The politics of valuing in information system construction. In *From data to action: Information systems in educational planning,* ed. D. Chapman and L. Mahlck, 92–116. Paris: International Institute for Educational Planning, UNESCO.

Welsh, T., and N. McGinn. 1996. Toward a methodology of stakeholder analysis. Cambridge, Mass.: Harvard Institute for International Development. Unpublished paper.

Whittington, D., and D. Macrae, Jr. 1986. The issue of standing in cost–benefit analysis. *Journal of Policy Analysis and Management* 5(4): 665–682.

Wicks, A. C., D. R. Gilbert, Jr., and R. E. Freeman. 1994. A feminist reinterpretation of the stakeholder concept. *Business Ethics Quarterly* 4(4): 475–497.

Wildavsky, A. B. 1975. *Budgeting: A comparative theory of budgetary processes.* Boston: Little, Brown.

Womack, J., D. Jones, and D. Roos. 1990. *The machine that changed the world.* New York: Macmillan.

Wong, K. 1993. Bureaucracy and school effectiveness. In *International encyclopedia of education,* ed. T. Husen and N. Postlethwaite, 589–594. Oxford: Pergamon Press.

World Bank. 1994. *El Salvador community education strategy: Decentralized school management.* Report No 13502-ES. Washington, D.C.: World Bank.

Index

ABOUT THE AUTHORS

FERNANDO REIMERS is a Policy Fellow (Education Specialist) at the Harvard Institute for International Development. On leave from Harvard he is currently serving as senior education specialist at the World Bank. He is coauthor (with D. Warwick) of *Hope or Despair: Learning in Pakistan's Primary Schools* (Praeger, 1995) and author of other books and articles on education and development. He has advised governments, universities and international agencies in 10 countries in Latin America, as well as in Egypt, Jordan and Pakistan.

NOEL McGINN is Professor of Education in the Graduate School of Education at Harvard University and Fellow (emeritus) at the Harvard Institute for International Development. He is coauthor (with R. G. King, R. Guerra, and D. Kline) of *The Provincial Universities of Mexico* (Praeger, 1979) and editor of *Crossing Lines: Research and Policy Networks for Developing Country Education* (Praeger, 1996). He has published many other books and articles on education and development. He has advised governments, universities, and research centers and international agencies in 24 countries in all continents on issues of education policy. He was the principal investigator of Project BRIDGES, a project funded by the United States Agency for International Development to research the determinants of student achievement in developing countries.